MONEY THERAPY

Money Therapy

How to start a love affair with money and transform your life

NICOLE RENEE

Nicole Renee Books

Nicole Renee Books
Pennsylvania

Copyright © 2024 by Nicole Renee

All rights reserved. No part of this book may be reproduced in any manner whatsoever without written permission from the author and publisher.

This work is solely for personal growth and education. It should not be treated as a substitute for professional assistance or financial advice. The application of protocols and information in this book is the choice of each reader, who assumes full responsibility for his or her understandings, interpretations, and results. The author and publisher assume no responsibility for the actions or choices of any reader.

All of the clinical examples in this book are composites. While the issues and interactions are accurate representations of Nicole Renee's work as a therapist, none of the examples refer to actual clients.

Money Therapy is a registered trademark.

Cover design by Deanna Seymour.

Printed in the United States of America

First Edition, 2024

For Tom, Elan, and Adley
*I love you more than the moon, more than the stars;
more than fireflies lighting up jars.*

Contents

INTRODUCTION: A BREAK UP & A BLIND DATE   1

PART I: THE CONSUMERISM TRAP

1	Consumerism	12
2	Neuromarketing	16
3	What Motivates Us to Consume?	19
4	Resisting Consumerism	26

Money Therapy Assignment   31

PART II: DESIRE: START A STEAMY LOVE AFFAIR WITH MONEY

5	Desire	34
6	Date Your Money	41
7	Money Dates	44
8	First Date Jitters	50
9	Old Money Baggage	58
10	Start Where You're At	60

Money Therapy Assignment   65

PART III: FALLING IN LOVE FOR KEEPS

11	Falling in Love for Keeps	68
12	Money Relationship Myths	73
13	Codependency	76
14	Cognitive Distortions	82

Money Therapy Assignment — 88

PART IV: MONEY PSYCHOLOGY 101

15	Using Your Mind as a Tool	96
16	Your Mind is Like a Puppy	104
17	Money Mindset	109
18	Your Mind is Like a Garden	112
19	Planting Your Money Garden	116

Money Therapy Assignment — 120

PART V: BELIEFS: SELF-WORTH DETERMINES NET WORTH

20	Toxic Money Beliefs	124
21	Feelings Aren't Facts	132
22	Rescripting Beliefs	137

Money Therapy Assignment — 141

PART VI: AN OUT-OF-BODY EXPERIENCE WITH MONEY

| 23 | A Little Bit of Woo-Woo | 144 |

24	Attracting Money	154
25	Money Manifesto	159
	Money Therapy Assignment	165

PART VII: MAKE UP OR BREAK UP

26	Make Up or Break Up	170
27	Bullying Your Money	173
28	Money Therapy	179
29	Restructuring Frustrations	183
	Money Therapy Assignment	187

PART VIII: THREATS TO THE MONEY RELATIONSHIP

30	Potential Threats to Your Money Relationship	190
31	Use Protection	198
32	Expectations and Agreements	202
33	Bringing Sexy Back	208
	Money Therapy Assignment	212

PART IX: MONEY MANAGEMENT-TAG TEAM IT WITH YOUR MONEY

34	Money Management Basics	216
35	Every Dollar Needs a Job	220
36	Buckets of Cash	222
37	Own It	226
38	Money Management Magic	228

	39	Automatic Lover	233
	40	Eliminate the Decision	238

Money Therapy Assignment — 240

PART X: PROTECTING YOUR MONEY MARRIAGE

	41	Prenuptial Agreement	244
	42	More than Dollars and Cents	248
	43	Home-wreckers	253
	44	Keeping Your Cash in Sickness & Health	260

Money Therapy Assignment — 262

PART XI: LIVING HAPPILY EVER AFTER WITH YOUR MONEY

	45	Happily Ever After?	266
	46	Money Fairy	270
	47	Take Your Money Out	275
	48	Be an Unstoppable Force of Good	278

Money Therapy Assignment — 281

PART XII: KEEPING THE SPARK ALIVE

	49	Happy Endings	284
	50	Repeating Stages	286
	51	Happily Ever After Defined	289
	52	Money Relationship Maintenance	291

Acknowledgments — 299

About The Author   301

INTRODUCTION: A BREAK UP & A BLIND DATE

Confession: I was a "bad girlfriend" to my money. I kept saying I wanted money to be around more and acted like I couldn't get enough of it, but I rarely made time to tend to my finances. I expected my money to give me what I wanted without willingly giving time and attention to it. I remember one night going out with my *very* wealthy girlfriend. She ordered three appetizers, lobster, and top-shelf drinks without batting an eye. Meanwhile, I began to sweat, worrying about how much she'd expect me to put toward the bill. We were both entrepreneurs, but she was a multi-millionaire, and I could barely pay my mortgage. Did she crack some secret money-making code? Or was I just a big, fat failure who didn't have what it takes to be rich? I wanted to give up on money, on my business, and on myself.

When the bill came, I held my breath in anticipation. Much to my relief, my girlfriend quickly grabbed it and insisted on treating that night. In that moment, I felt both gratitude and guilt. I could feel the shame, fear, and resentment I had about money bubble up to the surface. I didn't trust money to be there when I really needed it, and in my own mind, I talked smack about money all the time.

If money were a person, our relationship status would have been listed as "it's complicated." I didn't realize it at the time, but back in the day, I was a demanding jerk to my money. "Give me this! Give me that! Do this for me now!" No wonder my money never stuck around very long. It would come and go, leaving me feeling insecure and anxious. That "on again, off again" relationship was *not* my jam.

It wasn't until I experienced a messy, Jerry Springer-style financial crisis that I realized just how terrible my relationship with money truly was. But I'm getting ahead of myself.

Your Legit Money Therapist

I'm Nicole Renee; a Financial Therapist, Licensed Psychotherapist, and the creator of my trademarked program, *Money Therapy*. I earned a bachelor's degree in psychology; a master's degree in clinical social work; and have twenty years of experience working in mental health, Money Therapy, and business. I've been lucky to have done a bunch of cool, interesting things in my professional life, but most of my career has been spent doing individual and couple's therapy with clients at my mental health practice in Pennsylvania.

I never thought in a million years that I would find myself helping women deepen their relationship with money, earn more income, and manage money like a boss, but through a weird twist of fate, the Universe called me to do this work (much to my resistance).

As an ambitious entrepreneur, I wanted to take my mental health practice to the next level. So, in 2014, I decided to expand my business and create a full-service, holistic wellness center, complete with counseling, psychiatry, nutrition counseling, massage therapy, and yoga/fitness classes. I moved my business into an expensive building, paid for advertising, and hired contractors to provide additional services. I kept pouring money into the business, taking out additional loans to cover the monthly bills. I was $87,000 in debt and losing money in my business *every day*. The goal was always to be my own boss, change the world for the better, and make enough money to have financial security. But the reality was many sleepless nights worrying about the possibility of losing our house and feeling certain that owning a business that never turned a profit would prove I was a complete and utter failure.

How I tried to solve my money problems

In an act of desperation, I did what everyone does when they have a problem: went searching on Google. I typed "how to make more money" into the search bar and found advice on budgeting and investing in real estate. I found tools for money management and how to "win at the stock market." That wasn't going to work for me, at least not at that point in my life. I didn't have any money to budget! I didn't have the time to invest in real estate or the stock market and wait for it to produce a return. All I wanted was for someone to just tell me how to make some freakin' money right now!

When I was in that dark financial crisis, my greatest hope was to find an easy, step-by-step plan to make a boatload of money and get rich quickly. I wanted money, and fast, but I didn't want it to be short-lived and find myself right back where I started. I also didn't want to resort to sleazy, slimy sales tactics to make more money either. I wanted my financial troubles to be over for good while staying true to my values and ethics.

Then, as I reflected on my work as a couple's therapist, a lightbulb came on. I made a shocking discovery that my relationship with money was toxic. I was like a stage-four clinger who was totally obsessed with money but treated it like dirt when it was around. Then when money would run and hide from me, I would turn into a stalker, trying to get it back. My relationship with money looked a lot like the messed-up relationships my clients came in with, and that made me think about how I helped them turn it all around by teaching them to be kind and respectful, love up on each other, and make the relationship a priority.

Boom! That was it! That's exactly what I needed to do with my money relationship! I'd convinced hundreds of couples that the key to a happy marriage was giving their spouse really good reasons to stay. I desperately wanted my money to stick by me and work with me so we could have an awesome life together. My goals for money were the same goals as my clients had for their relationships! I figured that if I applied the strategies of couple's therapy to my relationship with money, we'd live happily ever after!

Why money is personified

My newfound awareness motivated me to start "dating my money." I consistently set aside quality time with my money, had "money dates", and loved up on my money so it would love me back. During those money dates, I asked many tough questions. Where the hell was all my money going? Why wasn't I making more money? What exactly did I want money for? If I had more money, what would I do with it? What did I value most in life? How much would it cost to live my dream life? Reflecting on these questions helped me clearly understand my values and what I wanted money to do for me.

Then I weighed every potential purchase against those values so I could make smarter buying decisions and spend less money on stupid, meaningless crap. That significantly reduced my expenses, and because of my budding love affair with money, money kept coming back more and more. My business revenue increased fivefold in eight months, and I paid off all $87,000 of my debt in two years.

My new love affair with money really started to blossom. I remember having weekend-long romantic getaways with my money where we'd eat chocolate-covered strawberries and dream of all the adventures we wanted to experience in the future. I used my money dates to set clear, long-term financial goals. I'd map out the income I wanted, when I wanted it, and what I'd do with all that beautiful money.

You might be wondering why I talk about money like a person, compare the money relationship to romantic relationships, and use figurative speech and metaphors to teach about money. Here's why. The mind gets tripped up when it tries to make sense of complicated or abstract concepts. **Money is one of those concepts.** Most people have complicated feelings and intense emotional responses about money, often because they just don't understand money. Personal finance can feel overwhelming, complicated, and intimidating when you don't understand how it all works.

We aren't taught about money in ways we can relate to, so our minds have a hard time making sense of it, and our lack of financial literacy creates big financial problems in our lives. Even when we seek help from a professional financial planner or advisor, we often feel dazed and confused as weird terms like "diversification," "asset allocation," and "compounding interest" are thrown around. It all seems so foreign and unfamiliar, and you walk away from those meetings frustrated that you don't know any more about money now than you did when you walked in. The worst part is that most financial professionals only focus on **what to do** with your money, not **how to think** or **feel differently** about money.

Money management is important, but the way you behave with money is completely influenced by your thoughts and feelings about money. If you have negative thoughts and feelings about money, those thoughts and feelings will undermine any steps you try to take toward making good decisions with your money. So, we gotta get in there and fix up your thoughts and feelings about money, and the first step is to understand more about money and the role it plays in your life.

You might also have concerns about your ability to manage your finances well. I often hear my clients say, "I'm bad with numbers, math, and money! I'll never figure this stuff out!" If you want to understand money, it has to be **relatable** instead of this weird, complicated, abstract thing. We have to compare money to something you're already familiar with, something you have experience with, something you already kind of understand—like a *romantic relationship*!

Your mind understands romantic relationships because you've likely experienced them before. If you haven't, you can draw from the other close relationships you've been in, like those with a parent, sibling, friend, or roommate. Drawing parallels between money and relationships takes a complicated concept and makes it easy to understand and digest. You also know and understand people, human attributes, and personality characteristics because you interact with people every day. People and personalities make sense.

Well, guess what? **You relate to and interact with money every day, too.** Every day, you think about money, make decisions about money, feel emotions related to money, and spend hours of your life working for money. You're in a relationship with anyone or anything you devote time, energy, and attention to, which means **you are in a relationship with money.** Now it's just a matter of figuring out what you want that relationship to look like.

You're probably here because you thought that being a grown-up meant you'd finally make the kind of money you want, but it isn't working out as you planned. Every time you look at your finances, you feel a sense of dread. Anxiety. Overwhelm. Nausea. You'd describe yourself as having a love/hate relationship with money, and you can't seem to figure out what your wealthy neighbors are doing differently from you.

You wish someone would help, but who do you turn to? You don't exactly want to admit to your friends what's going on in your bank account. Your spouse/partner/lover? Whole 'nother drama. You'd love to talk to a professional, but financial planners only look at the hardcore numbers, not the emotions you feel around them.

What you need is Money Therapy. And needing Money Therapy doesn't mean there's anything wrong with you or that you suck at money. It means that money matters are hard and you're human. You aren't given a manual for creating a healthy relationship with money, instructions on how to earn your worth, or tutorials on how to manage money like a boss. You've been left to figure it out as you go, probably making lots of mistakes along the way (*raises hand*). Or you're approaching money the same way your parents did (for better or worse).

That's what Money Therapy^R is for. The goal of this book is to help you think and feel better about money so you can behave better with money. It's to improve your relationship with money so you can improve your entire financial life. And as your legit financial therapist, I'll be right here guiding you through every step of the Money Therapy^R process, so you can create a steamy love affair with money and live the life of your dreams.

How to read this book

Before we dive in, let me explain how this book is structured and why so you can get the most out of the reading experience. Almost everyone I've ever worked with wants to start with money management. I often hear, "Just tell me what to do with my money." I don't like focusing on behaviors first because our thoughts and feelings unconsciously influence our behaviors. So, this book starts by sharing some important things you should know about psychology and what influences the ways you behave with money.

I suggest reading this book in sequential order, as each part and chapter builds on the previous one. The book walks you through the various stages of the money relationship, step-by-step. As such, please resist the temptation to skip ahead.

I realize that you're a very busy woman, you haven't got all day, and you're carving time out of your busy schedule to love up on your money by reading this book (and I'm so proud of you for doing so!). So, I've separated each section of the book into bite-size pieces to prevent overwhelm and make it easy for you to read short bits while you're waiting in line at the grocery store or squeezing in some light reading over your lunch break.

At the end of each part, you'll find a Money Therapy assignment to complete. These assignments help you take action and apply what you've learned, which is the key to improving your financial life and healing your relationship with money. Homework helps you hardwire new skills, reflect, gain awareness, and experiment with new solutions to old problems. Each assignment can be completed in under an hour.

Now we're ready to get this party started! Settle in. Make yourself comfortable and get ready to get *uncomfortable*. We're starting this money love story with something that may surprise you and could very well be hurting your money relationship in this very moment: **consumerism**.

PART I: THE CONSUMERISM TRAP

Chapter 1

Consumerism

I rarely watch TV. One day, out of sheer boredom, I flipped on the tube and scrolled through the channels. All commercials. With nothing better to watch, I sat through the seven-minute series of advertisements. On comes a Coca-Cola ad that features a close-up of an ice-cold glass of Coke. I heard the clinking of the ice cubes and the fizzing of the soda bubbles. The bright colors, fun music, and happy vibes of that Coke ad had me in a trance. My mouth started watering, and all I could think about was getting my hands on a Coke. I shook my head to snap out of it. What just happened? I don't even like soda! Why in the world did I, all of a sudden, want to immediately run to the store for a Coke?

Perhaps you've experienced this same phenomenon. You see an advertisement, and something clicks. You suddenly want that thing like no other. You'll walk through fire to get it. You'll spend whatever money you have to. You want it, and you want it NOW! So, what is this magical spell that comes over us and makes us feel like a superhero, ready to unleash our shopping powers on the next Nordstrom we walk into?

It's consumerism, my friend. Consumerism is an economic theory that states that it's beneficial to consumers (you and me) to have a progressively greater level of consumption of goods and services. In short, it's a constant, in-your-face message that:

- More is better.
- Companies know what's best for you and have the solutions to your problems.
- Having whatever they're selling will make you happy.

Consumerism in itself is not a bad thing, but the ways you consume can have serious consequences for your wallet. We often buy more stuff to feel happy, fulfilled, and confident. Those feelings are usually short-lived. Consuming more often leads to feeling empty, devoid of meaning, and chronically cranky. If you lack awareness about your own consuming behaviors and the correlated effects of your buying habits, you might find yourself in a perpetual cycle of retail therapy followed by buyer's remorse.

My client, "Allison," had always struggled with her weight. In her teen years, she started trying every fad diet under the sun, hoping to drop the weight for good and feel confident in her own skin. As she approached the age of forty, she felt defeated. She resigned herself to accept that she'd never be as slim as she'd like and started settling.

As a divorced mother of two young kids, she started online dating in hopes of finding her "forever person." This was incredibly difficult for her at first because she hadn't been on a first date in over fifteen years and she wasn't sure how men would feel about her weight when they saw her in person. She felt like she needed to go the extra mile to look her best, so she'd have a chance at finding love again. She couldn't stand the thought of spending another four years single and lonely.

Allison set out on a mission to look her best for every date she went on. She bought designer clothes and sparkly jewelry to match, hoping the gems around her neck would distract from the extra cushion around her waist. She religiously got her nails done every week and a cut and color every six weeks. She justified each swipe of her credit card by telling herself that she wouldn't have a chance with anyone if she didn't look like the stylish women she saw in magazines.

And there were a lot of dates with a lot of different men. A pattern quickly formed. She would meet a new guy, fall hard and fast, and spend hundreds of dollars to make herself look her best to keep him around. Then, after a few months, each guy would lose interest or reveal a huge flaw, causing the relationship to end abruptly.

Not only was this emotionally painful for Allison, but it was also hurting her financial health as well. One day, she looked at her credit card bills and realized she'd racked up almost $10,000 of debt by trying to make herself look good for dates. She'd even gone as far as borrowing from her mother because she'd maxed out all the credit cards she had. Allison stared at a closet packed full of clothes and felt ashamed of herself for spending so much money on them, only to find herself still without the relationship she truly wanted.

Allison was trying to cover up her insecurities about her weight with material objects. She was literally buying into the idea that designer clothes and acrylic nails would make her more lovable, but her impulsive spending habits were making her feel even more insecure, unworthy, and out of control. The cycle continued as she tried numbing her self-doubt and desperation for companionship with retail therapy and expensive beauty rituals.

In turn, Allison's relationship with her mother started to suffer because of the money she'd borrowed from her. Feeling guilty and embarrassed about not paying her mother back, Allison started working overtime to make extra money to pay her debts. After several months of overtime shifts, her kids really started missing her and began acting out as a way to get her attention. This only added to Allison's stress and guilt.

Allison's underlying low self-esteem was the root of the problem, and her lack of self-worth had a tremendous impact on her life. She was unhappy in her body and in her life. She coped by numbing the pain with shopping, hiding her body under expensive clothes, and turning to magazines and billboards for inspiration on what beauty looks like so she could emulate more confident women and snag a man. She was completely unaware that consumerism, combined with neuromarketing, influenced her decisions and contributed to the financial strain she felt every day.

Chapter 2

Neuromarketing

Neuromarketing uses medical technologies such as functional Magnetic Resonance Imaging (fMRI) to study the brain's responses to advertisements. FMRI scans measure the amount of oxygenated blood in the brain. When an area of the brain is working hard, it needs more blood to fuel it. So, when our brains start kicking into overdrive at the sight of a product we're attracted to, blood increases in that region of the brain and lights up on a fMRI scan.

If we'd scanned Allison's brain, we'd have seen bursts of activity when she flipped through the slick, glossy pages of fashion magazines. When Allison looked at advertisements for the sexy perfume that would "drive a man wild" and the bold, red lip color that would "make his heart beat a little faster," her brain went wild with desire. She made an association between the advertised products and experiencing pleasure (snagging the man of her dreams). Her mind was saying, "Yes! That's what I need! I want a man and those things will help me get one!" Of course, she wasn't aware that was what was happening. All she knew is that she wanted it because the ad had convinced her that the product would solve her loneliness.

The use of sophisticated technology, like fMRI, is what makes neuromarketing research different from standard market research studies. When consumers are given surveys, for example, they are often asked about their reasons for buying a particular product. The problem with this method is that most people don't know the real reason behind why they buy what they buy. As we saw with Allison, most purchasing decisions are unconscious and based on feelings rather than rational thoughts, making it nearly impossible for market researchers to gather accurate data that can be used to influence future purchasing choices.

This is why neuromarketing is so appealing to companies; it provides them with an insider's look into our brains and gives them precise data. Big companies hire neuroscientists to share information about the inner workings of the mind with them so they can develop strong marketing and advertising campaigns that our brains won't be able to resist, essentially manipulating our buying habits and getting us to buy more and more of what they have to offer. Sounds freaky, right?

That Coke commercial was strategically designed and engineered to trick my mind into craving a Coke, and it totally worked! I would've given in to the temptation had I not been aware of how consumerism is like a sex addiction: wanting more and more without ever feeling satisfied. Similarly, a shopaholic goes out and splurges, thinking all those material objects will satisfy her cravings or fill the void, but she's still left wanting. Meanwhile, her poor money just can't keep up. All it wants is to snuggle up with her and get some attention instead of her "blowing it" all the time (pun intended).

Chapter 3

What Motivates Us to Consume?

The consumerism/neuromarketing combo doesn't just put us under a spell, making us believe that more is better and the only way to be happy is to have more stuff. An important part of the consumption process is that we have to be motivated to buy. So what motivates us to consume?

Desire and pleasure. Seeking pleasure gets us closer to experiencing the feelings we desire. Avoiding pain works in the same way. So, our brains are constantly scanning the environment, searching for opportunities to experience pleasure and avoid pain. This entire process is greatly influenced by our core beliefs.

Pleasure comes in many forms and some are *expensive*. Ah, the pleasure of shopping. Touching all the things with your hands, holding them, smelling them, dreaming about what it would be like to take them home. Imagining yourself all wrapped up in that hot, sexy...sweater. Gazing longingly as you imagine the feel of the pulsing vibrations moving up and down your spine. How good it will feel to have that...back massager. And it's on sale. How can you possibly say "no"? You can't. You say "yes" and walk out of Brookstone with a $100 back massager. You go home, savor your ten-minute back massage, and then remember you have to get your car serviced and inspected this month. Crap! You just spent that money on the back massager! But the massager feels so good. But the crunch for money hurts. The pleasure...the pain...it hurts so good. How can that be?

You see, your brain is always seeking *pleasure* and trying to avoid *pain*. When I'm having a really crappy day or when I've cranked out some serious productivity and feel like I should be rewarded with a treat, I immediately start scanning the environment to find what will bring me a hit of pleasure. It's not a conscious thing. I do it without even thinking about it. My mind goes on the prowl for the thing that's going to make me feel oh-so-good. Because I'm a hardcore coffee addict, that's usually what gets me my fix. Mmm...a hot cup of pleasure just for me! A cup of coffee here and there doesn't seem like a big deal, but when you spend five bucks a cup at Starbucks on the regular, it becomes a big deal for your wallet. I would know.

In his book, *Buy-ology*, Martin Lindstrom explains that trying to avoid pain can be just as expensive. Lindstrom states that neuromarketing scientists have discovered six basic fears that most people have: fear of poverty, criticism, ill health, loss of a loved one, old age, and death. Companies appeal to these fears by offering solutions to each problem in subtle, yet compelling, advertising campaigns. "Feeling afraid of old age as you notice all those new gray hairs and wrinkles? Avoid the fear of getting old with this new root-color touch-up gel and anti-aging face cream!" If you examine every piece of marketing out there, you'll find that it either addresses what we desire and makes a promise to bring us the pleasure we seek ("These new multivitamins will give you more energy, boost your immune system, and improve your skin!") or addresses our fears and offers a solution to our current or future problems ("You want to be around to walk your daughter down the aisle, so take these multivitamins every day for longevity and good health!").

Dopamine is the second motivator. It's one of the brain's pleasure chemicals and one of the most addictive substances known to man. When you see that shiny watch or the designer handbag, dopamine is released in your brain, providing pleasure, which motivates you to max out the credit card. The decision to purchase happens in as little as two seconds. Then, a few minutes later, you'll leave the store, bag in hand, and the euphoric feelings caused by the dopamine rush will subside, making you want to cry into your vanilla latte for spending that money. Sound familiar?

This dopamine addiction is commonly referred to as "retail therapy." We spend a lot of our free time shopping for anything. We shop for clothes, home furnishings, diet programs, gym memberships, and food. We even shop for romantic partners and sex these days. But does all this shopping (a.k.a. consumerism) make us happier? Scientifically, yes, but only in the short term. Once the dopamine is done and gone, we go back to our original feeling state. And, sometimes, we experience buyer's remorse and actually feel worse.

Dopamine addiction has become prevalent in our society, largely due to technological advancements, which make it easier than ever to get a dopamine fix. Buying is easier now that we have online markets to provide us with products delivered right to our door within forty-eight hours. No longer do we have to experience the inconvenience (pain) of getting dressed and going out in public to get a hit of dopamine in our brains. Nope. We can stay in our jammies, safe in the comfort of our homes, and get our shopping fixes with the click of a button.

In fact, our computers are constantly scouring the internet in search of products we might like. Ever notice how you do a Google search one day and find thirty ads promoting products on that topic the next? That's neuromarketing and targeted advertising at its best! You don't even have to go to the trouble of looking for goods and services yourself. Advertisers do all the work for you and offer a steady stream of ads to your social media feeds and email inboxes, making it incredibly simple to get the rush of dopamine that feels so good.

Have you ever run to the store for one little thing, like toilet paper or tampons, but left the store with a cart full of goodies? Did you ever pack your lunch so you could save money, only to ditch the brown bag for Panera's autumn squash soup, turkey panini, a cookie, and a coffee...walking out $15 poorer? If your hand is raised (mine certainly is!), then you love quickies! These quickies, brief acts of impulsive spending, are addicting. They're quick, easy, and fun. Total pleasure bombs. You get a dopamine rush. Immediate gratification. No waiting or wanting. It's yours. NOW.

But you probably know from experience that quickies don't help your money relationship. While impulsive spending, buying things in the moment that you didn't intend to buy, feels good for a hot second, it doesn't feel good after the fact. It especially doesn't feel good to your money. So, if you want to keep your money happy, you'll want to trade in your love of quickies for a slow and steady approach.

The third and final factor that influenced Allison's buying decisions (and everyone's) is mirror neurons. They play a big part in motivating you to buy more and more. Mirror neurons are neurons in the brain that fire when you observe what other people are doing and then you copy them. You see their behavior and do the exact same thing.

What this means is that humans are biologically predisposed to mimic each other. We do it without thinking about it. It happens automatically, and we rarely even know that it's occurring. Have you ever noticed that when you're around someone who's positive, upbeat, and enthusiastically tackling life's challenges, you tend to feel on top of the world and ready for anything? Or maybe you've spent a lot of time around someone who likes to smoke while out at the bar, and, before you know it, you catch yourself bumming cigarettes from strangers whenever you're with her. You see, moods are contagious (for better or worse), all because of mirror neurons. We emulate one another's behaviors and even adopt each other's feelings and mindsets.

This applies to consumerism, too. When we encounter people we admire or envy, our mirror neurons go wild, and we become motivated to be just like them. When we see sexy Victoria Secret models, we fill our bags with lingerie that will make us look just like that! Jennifer Aniston shows off her glowing skin in the Olay commercial, and we need that cream so our skin can look as youthful as hers! We look up to the CEO of our company and find ourselves shopping at the same stores she does, so we can have that same powerful look.

The truth is that mirror neurons radically affect our buying habits. Have you ever seen a product you just didn't like at all? Maybe a pair of shoes, a jacket, or skinny jeans? But then you started seeing that item everywhere, and suddenly those shoes you found hideous are the same shoes you just can't live without now.

Sometimes seeing a product over and over again can make it more appealing to us because our brain is naturally inclined to mimic other people. So, if everyone is wearing skinny jeans, you're going to start wearing them too, even if at first you hated them. As you can see, imitation is a huge factor in why we buy what we buy.

This is what the phrase, "Keeping Up with the Joneses," refers to. Thanks to mirror neurons, we want to be like everyone else. We want to have a sense of belonging. This desire to fit in can lead to a competition of who has more and who has better.

By knowing the top three things that motivate us to consume (desire, dopamine, and mirror neurons), you can see how little influence and control we have when it comes to making purchasing decisions. We can't always control our desires; we want what we want. You have no influence or control over when your brain releases dopamine or how your mirror neurons fire.

Furthermore, most of our buying decisions aren't even remotely conscious. Our subconscious mind makes most of the purchasing decisions, and we aren't even aware of it. Then cognitive distortions start popping up and add a dose of irrationality to the mix, which you'll learn more about later in this book. Neuromarketing motivates us to go for the external win at the cost of our financial wellness; it drives us to seek outer attainment rather than inner attunement.

As an example of how irrational our buying decisions can be, research studies have found that the saying "you get what you pay for" seems to be deeply rooted in our minds. When presented with two identical items (like bottles of wine), people are actually more likely to choose the one that has the higher price. Our mind perceives the higher price to mean greater value, which isn't necessarily true. Think about how much money your irrational mind is costing you!

As consumers, we're often unaware of how our mind affects our consumption. However, the companies that are marketing and selling products to us know all about how the mind works because of neuromarketing. Thus, they have the power to manipulate us to consume more.

Chapter 4

Resisting Consumerism

So, how can you maintain your strength and keep your hard-earned cash in your wallet when consumerism and neuromarketing are manipulating your mind to spend it? The first step is to always be skeptical. Be skeptical of every advertisement, every commercial, every new trend, and even every desire that pops up in your mind that says, "Oh, I just have to have that!" Don't always believe the experts or the ads.

Millions of dollars are spent each year on neuromarketing research that tells companies exactly how to appeal to you and get you to buy more and more of what they're dangling in front of you. Now that you know this, you're no longer a clueless shopper ready to whip out the Visa and sign your life away. Use this newfound awareness and question whether or not you really want the thing you're tempted to buy.

Consumerism can absolutely destroy your life by eating up your money and tricking you into "quick fixes" that make you feel good for a bit and then wear off. Remember, you aren't always consciously aware of what's going on in your mind, and many of your buying decisions aren't made through conscious, rational thought. Buying decisions are made by the irrational part of your mind (hello there, Ego) that wants to get a rush of pleasure. Knowing how consumerism and neuromarketing work in tandem is incredibly valuable because it allows you to challenge those irrational thoughts before acting on them.

I've experienced the destructive power of consumerism firsthand. The suffering that it caused me is what led to my breakup and make-up with money. My workaholism developed from erroneously thinking that working harder, longer hours made me a more valuable member of society. My addiction to achievement and productivity worsened in adulthood as I got sucked into the cog of consumerism, believing that making more money and buying fancier stuff would prove I'm worthy. Worthy of what, I wasn't quite sure.

Over time, I grew tired of working for other people. As an overachiever, I often felt like I was putting in more than I was getting out of any job, and my hatred for bureaucracy motivated me to become my own boss. Starting my own private practice felt like a far-off dream, but when my husband and I learned we were pregnant, I decided to move closer to my family. I found myself in a new town, unable to get a job in my field. I felt I had no other choice than to create a job for myself. My private practice was born, and I started working as a psychotherapist with adult individuals and couples. What should have felt like a success was actually a source of stress and financial strain. I needed to spend money to promote and advertise my business before I could make money, and I had none.

Over time, things slowly improved, and I started making money, but very little and certainly not what I deserved. While I loved the work I was doing and the freedom of working for myself, my salary paled in comparison to when I was an employee. I had no benefits, no paid time off, and no certainty of what my paycheck would look like from one week to the next. Yet, I still tried to maintain the lifestyle I lived when I'd been working two or three jobs at once.

I continued to shop at Ann Taylor and Banana Republic. I continued to add to my collection of Coach bags and went out to eat just as often as before. After all, the advertisements were directly appealing to my pleasure sensors, and my lack of awareness kept me trapped in a cycle of retail therapy. I used my credit cards as I always had, but I no longer paid off the balance in full when the statement came. I watched the balances grow higher and higher and told myself I would start making more money soon, and it would all be okay.

It wasn't okay. In fact, it got worse before it got better. I decided that I wanted to expand my business by adding additional services and hiring staff. I thought this was the answer to my "making no money but working my ass off" woes. Society and consumerism had adequately trained me to believe that having more money would be the answer to all my problems. I became obsessed with making more money and wouldn't stop until I found out how to do it.

Maybe that's where you're at now. Perhaps your financial struggles are driving you to find the answers that will make it rain money. During that time of financial despair, my greatest hope was to find an easy way to make a boatload of money and get rich quick. Here again, consumerism had led me to believe that getting rich quickly was actually a possibility and that I could only be happy if I had more money, more luxuries to enjoy, and higher status to show off. For years, I had seen stories, marketing gimmicks, and product advertisements cross my social media pages and email inbox telling me that "this new method for attracting clients was the answer to my prayers" and "this new home-based business would triple my income." I was led to believe that if I paid a thousand dollars for the online program they offered, they'd show me exactly how they turned their failing business into a multi-million-dollar venture. I fell for many of those promises, trying anything possible to make more money, only to find they were empty.

The truth stung. There's no way to get rich quick, and if there were, it certainly wouldn't be sustainable income that I could depend on. I wanted more money, and fast, but I wasn't willing to sacrifice my integrity to get it, nor was I willing to work ninety hours a week or sell my soul to a corporate job I'd hate.

It wasn't until I became my own client and started doing Money Therapy^R with myself that I was able to gain awareness about what it really takes to make more money. It had nothing to do with hustling and grinding at work or manipulating people to hand over fistfuls of cash. It didn't involve wanting to keep up with the Joneses or impress people with status symbols. Everything that I taught my clients in couple's therapy was the exact opposite of consumerism and focused on nurturing the relationship with time, attention, compassion, and love. Tending to my money relationship with love, respect, gratitude, and appreciation was the hidden answer to making more money: an answer that didn't pop up on a Google search.

My awareness of consumerism and how it affected my money relationship helped me to break free from the "more is better" trap. I began by spending money only on what I truly valued rather than the stuff society told me I was supposed to want. Getting crystal clear on your values is an important first step in healing your relationship with money and involves introspection and self-reflection. If you don't know what you value, it's impossible to live in alignment with those values. If you don't live in alignment with your values, you'll be really unhappy because the mind doesn't like incongruence. Our thoughts and behaviors must match up. Furthermore, if you aren't clear on what you value and truly want, you'll fall victim to consumerism and buy whatever the advertisements say will make you happy. You already know what that outcome is.

Your best defense against consumerism and neuromarketing is to be aware of them. Be skeptical of advertisements so they don't put you in a trance and pressure you to cheat on your money.

Money Therapy Assignment

Analyzing Ads: practicing awareness and skepticism of advertisements

Turn on the television and watch until you see an advertisement that appeals to you; one that makes you want to buy what it's selling. Turn off the TV and analyze the advertisement by answering the following questions:

1. What was the product being advertised?
2. Had you thought about buying that product prior to seeing the ad?
3. What colors, sounds, or images stood out to you?
4. What did you find most appealing? What caught your attention right away?
5. If there were people in the ad, what were they doing? How do you think they were feeling in the ad?
6. What do you think the advertisers were trying to make *you* feel while watching it?
7. Were the advertisers successful in making you feel that way? How did the ad make you feel?
8. How do you think you'd feel if you had what the ad was promoting?
9. How does the product fit in with your values in life?

10. Now that you've analyzed the ad, are you still interested in buying the product?

By having more awareness and skepticism of advertisements, you'll be better able to resist consumerism. This will save you boatloads of money and will reduce the amount of clutter you have in your home, creating better organization and peace. It will also help you only buy the things you really want rather than wasting your precious resources on things that don't really matter.

PART II: DESIRE: START A STEAMY LOVE AFFAIR WITH MONEY

Chapter 5

Desire

Get ready for some excitement because we're going to dive right in with a smokin' hot topic. That's right; we're going to figure out what your heart is longing for and use your passion to kickstart a love affair with money.

Have you ever noticed the pattern that most human beings develop when it comes to spending money? In a society driven by consumerism, we find ourselves seeing something we want, working countless hours to gain the resources to get it, and then once we have it, we're still left wanting. How does this happen? Wouldn't it be reasonable to believe that once you reach a goal you've set for yourself (getting what you want) you'd be really happy? So why is this so often not the case?

Your desires are revealing. If you listen closely, your desires will whisper that you want this thing because it will make you feel complete. Or that you want that thing because it will make you feel powerful. Or that you want the other thing because it will make you feel free.

The truth is you don't really want that *thing*. You want the *feeling* that "thing" will bring you. Most people don't really care about the new Fitbit or Apple's latest iPhone or the shiny Volvo plastered on every billboard. What they care about is feeling healthy and strong when the Fitbit tracks their steps for the day. They yearn to be connected to the people they love, be free to express their opinions on social media any time of the day, and be energized while listening to their favorite tunes on their iPhone. They want the feelings of power, speed, and status that come with the car.

Wanting these things—I mean, feelings—isn't bad or wrong, so don't go labeling yourself as materialistic or greedy. Some say that the purpose of life is happiness, and I tend to agree. Now, this isn't to say that the car or iPhone will make you blissfully happy or solve all your problems. Advertisers try to make you believe that's the case, but it isn't.

Really, you'll only be happy if you *feel* what you want to feel by obtaining that possession or experience. Yes, in a way, possessions can bring you happiness, if they create the feeling you desire. Life is meant to be enjoyed. If you truly desire to feel complete, powerful, and free, then you should absolutely feel that way—but you need to question whether that thing will actually bring you those feelings or not.

This starts with knowing what you *really* want. Diving in deep to identify your heart's desires is critical for living the life you want. It's essential to tap into the emotions you want to feel because without desire, you won't be motivated enough to create, design, love, care for, heal, help, build, learn, or teach *anything*. You must have a crystal-clear vision of the dream life you want to live. No ambiguous, "I'm-not-really-sure-what-I-want" nonsense. Lack of clarity on what it is you *desire* and how you truly want to *feel* can lead to financial ruin for several reasons:

• If you're currently feeling bad and don't know what will make you feel good, you're more likely to spend money aimlessly searching for the "thing" that will make you feel better. (And chances are, nothing money can buy will cut it for you, and you'll end up with nothing but a boatload of debt.)

• If you don't know what you desire, you'll have no sense of direction. You'll just be floating along aimlessly, feeling lost and unfulfilled. And since you don't have a plan for your money, you'll probably make some bad decisions with it along the way.

• If you focus on reaching a goal but don't consider the feeling you're after, you might hustle to get there only to find yourself feeling empty and unsatisfied despite all your hard work. For example, if you have no clue what it will feel like to pay off your student loans, you won't work your tail off to accomplish that goal. If you aren't clear about wanting to feel freedom, independence, and security, you won't religiously contribute to your retirement account every month. If you don't feel the burning desire to experience complete rest, relaxation, and peace, there's no way you're going to sock away the necessary funds for the beach home you dream of.

Now, you might be asking yourself, "How do I know if the thing I want will result in the desired feeling?" I wish I could tell you that there's an exact science to this process that guarantees the possessions or experiences you *think* you want will create the *feelings* you want, but that's not the case. It's more about making educated guesses. The beach home you dream of might provide the feeling of complete relaxation you're after or it might become a source of stress if people are constantly hounding you to stay there. You won't know exactly how you'll feel until you have the thing, which is why it's a smart move to try the least expensive and/or least time-consuming option first.

For example, you might not want to spend the next ten years working and saving for the beach house to feel relaxed and calm. Maybe you test out your theory first by saving for a month-long stay at a beach rental to see if it brings you the feeling you're after. You could also try other less expensive options to achieve feelings of rest and relaxation, like chilling by a friend's pool or spending the day at the lake. Experimenting to see if the possession you desire will bring about the feeling you want is always a good idea, but even then, you can't always predict exactly how you'll feel.

Let me give you an example from my own life. I've never had a new car, or a fancy one, or one that's anything above the base model. Every vehicle I've ever driven (a whopping total of three) has been pre-owned and extremely basic. I could never afford more than that.

My Mitsubishi Endeavor was my favorite. It was safe, reliable, and perfect for hauling around dogs, kids, and large home-improvement supplies, which is probably why I drove it for twelve years! But as much as I appreciated its good qualities, I secretly wished it were a shiny, black Audi Q7 with leather interior, sunroof, and heated seats. Yet, I knew I'd never be able to afford a car like that, or at least that's what I thought back then.

Once I got clear on my desires and became fully committed to my money relationship, mind-blowing financial transformations occurred. I created a healthy, nurturing, and fun relationship with money and restructured my limiting money beliefs. I started using a spending plan that showed me how much money I had and where it was going, and I stuck to the freaking budget so I didn't go into debt. I paid off all my debt to avoid the living paycheck-to-paycheck cycle of doom. I began saving and investing to make my money work for me instead of working more hours to get ahead financially.

As a result of making those money changes, I was able to make the most indulgent, expensive purchase of my life. I bought a shiny, black 2017 Audi Q7 with the freaking leather interior, sunroof, and heated seats! I felt excitement and joy because I'd waited so long for this car, and now I finally had it! It's what I wanted for years. It was a dream come true.

I felt successful and accomplished. Every time I sat in the Audi, I felt like I'd made it. I felt proud that the hard work I poured into my business and my money relationship paid off. All of those desired feelings motivated me to buy the Audi in the first place.

I also felt something completely unexpected: guilt and shame. My inner critic chimed in: "Who do you think you are, getting something like this? How materialistic of you to spend so much on a car. What did you do to deserve something so great? What will other people think of you now?" Ouch. The feelings that surfaced caught me off-guard. I started to worry about what other people would think about my new car. Would they see me as materialistic? Would they see me as a "rich bitch"? Or arrogant? Or selfish? Or entitled? Did I see those qualities in myself? Did I buy the Audi to prove something or "keep up with the Joneses"?

This train of thought unleashed some hardcore self-reflection. Here's what I discovered: My most indulgent purchase ever revealed I still had A LOT of inner work to do when it came to my money beliefs. Clearly, I still had limiting beliefs about my own self-worth and what I truly deserved. I'm a work in progress just like everyone else. Don't expect yourself to have it all figured out either. It's all about the journey, not the destination.

I also learned that caring about what other people think of me is a great way to ruin joy. Concerning myself with other people's opinions ripped away the excitement I'd felt initially. So, I cut that crap out. You might find that once you start attracting the material possessions you want in life that people will start judging you, but don't let that keep you from having the things you want. People will always judge you for something, and it's none of your business what other people think. The only thing that matters is what *you* think.

The unpleasant feelings I experienced helped me to realize that having nice things doesn't change who I am. I had to remind myself of my true essence. I'm kind, generous, and down-to-earth. I needed to push out all the false messages about possessions defining who I am by rescripting unhealthy beliefs (which you'll learn how to do in this book). This is important to keep in mind as you attract your desires. The car you drive, the house you live in, and the clothes you wear don't define who you are. Your thoughts and actions make you who you are. Money doesn't change you; it merely amplifies what's already there.

Lastly, my Audi purchasing experience reminded me that material things don't make us happy, but we can experience happiness from material things. I didn't buy the Audi so I could be happy; I was already happy when I bought it. But having it made me feel even happier in certain ways.

However, I didn't know with certainty how I'd feel before I bought the Audi. I made an educated guess that having it would bring about feelings of excitement, success, and accomplishment, and in my case, I was right. Had I been wrong though, I would have felt terrible about spending so much money and not feeling the way I wanted to. If that had happened, I probably would have sold the Audi and gone back to exploring my desires to gain better insight into what I truly wanted. We'll talk more about how to gain clarity on desires later on.

Don't let a lack of clarity about what you really want keep you from being happy. Your desires will be the map that will govern how and where you spend your money, time, energy, and attention, and you'll need to constantly refer to that map to make sure you're on track. Asking yourself about what you want and why you want it uncovers your highest priorities and values. So ask yourself: How much money do I want to make? Why do I want to make that much? What will I do with that money? How will I feel when the money is in my hands?

These questions will stir up a variety of emotions for you. You might feel hopeless that you'll never have the money you want. You might feel undeserving of money. Maybe feelings of excitement, fear, anxiety, anticipation, worry, or overwhelm are popping up for you. Then again, digging into your deepest desires might make you start fantasizing about the kind of love story you could have with your money. It might make you feel weak in the knees and totally smitten with your money. After all, money can make life so much easier and provide you with the pleasures you dream of. Right? Let's find out by fanning the flame on your money relationship!

Chapter 6

Date Your Money

Before I admitted to myself that I was a bad girlfriend to money, I held a lot of resentment toward it; it was truly a love/hate relationship. I had big dreams of changing the world, and I needed money to help me do it. I wanted to live a healthier, more fulfilling life than I saw my family of origin live, and again, I needed money to help me live the way I wanted. At the time, I didn't realize how awful I treated my money. Looking back, I can see why money wanted to get away from me.

I wasn't faithful to my money. I would make promises that I wouldn't overspend. I vowed to remain loyal to the plans I'd made with my money in my budget. Then, instead of setting aside money in my emergency fund as I'd planned, I cheated on my money with splurges at Target and Barnes & Noble. The vicious cycle of retail therapy followed by buyer's remorse landed me $87,000 in debt. I'd lie awake at night and worry about how to pay the bills. I was struggling to make enough money in my business to keep the doors open. No wonder money never stuck around very long. I abused and neglected my money. And because of that, it would come and go, leaving me feeling insecure and anxious.

If I'd treated my husband the same way I treated money, he would've packed his bags and bolted. I know this with certainty because I've witnessed it happen with other couples from my therapist chair. But I would never dream of nagging at my husband the way I did with my money. No way. I adore him and want nothing more than to have fun with him, play around like we're kids again, and relax and laugh with him.

That's exactly what my money wanted to do with me! It's what money wants to do with you! It doesn't want the relationship to feel intimidating or scary. It doesn't want you freaking out every time a bill comes in the mail or pulling your hair out as you stare at boring spreadsheets. Your money wants you to make it a priority and spend quality time with it, like having a date with your money. The money relationship is meant to feel fun and flirty!

Before I started Money Therapy[R], I gave all my attention to chasing money by hustling and grinding in my business and spent more time shuffling through stacks of bills and biting my nails than I did showering my money with gratitude. I remember opening up my bank statement one day and bursting into tears, feeling panicked and wondering how I would pay the bills with such little money.

Instead of taking time to see what was working (or, at that time, *not* working) in my money relationship and putting in the effort to make it better, I sat there feeling sorry for myself because I didn't have the money I wanted. I focused on what was going wrong instead of what could go right. Most of all, I blamed money. It was all money's fault.

It was never there when I needed it. I couldn't count on it. That good-for-nothing S.O.B.

It took me a while to see it, but I was being a total hypocrite. How many times did I teach couples to look for the good in their relationships? If I had a dollar for every time I put the kibosh on couples throwing blame at each other in my office, all my money troubles would be over! Yet, I was doing the exact same thing in my own money relationship.

I jumped back into the therapist's chair, became my own client, and gently confronted myself. I told myself to do what I ask my couple's therapy clients to do: go on dates. MONEY DATES.

Chapter 7

Money Dates

Simply put, a money date is time you intentionally set aside for your money to love up on it, flirt and play with it, check in on it, and catch up with it. It's quality time between you and your money to nurture the relationship, make plans for the future, and express your appreciation for all the things money does for you. Every day, you make money, spend money, or decide what to do with your money. As such, you're in a relationship with your money, and, like it or not, you *need* money.

Think of it like this: your life is like a car; money is like fuel, and your dreams are all the destinations you want to visit on your journey. Sure, you could push the car to each dreamy destination, but that would take forever, totally exhaust you, and wear holes in your Jimmy Choos. Money fuels your life and gets you to where you want to go faster and easier. And let's be real; money makes life better because it gives you the power to change the world and make other people's lives better too.

Money can and will give you your heart's desires if you're good to it. Wanna tour around Thailand on a beach cruiser bike and volunteer at an elephant sanctuary? You need money to get there. Yearning for a twenty-hour work week so you have ample time and energy to care for your babies? Money makes it possible. Dreaming of starting a scholarship fund for BIPOC women who want to study fine art in college or wishing you could provide in-home care for your aging grandparents? Money makes dreams come true. Maybe your heart's desires are to go to Bali on a yoga retreat, put your kids through college so they don't start out with a boatload of debt, and soak in a hot tub on your back patio on a chilly fall night. Money can provide all those things if you respect it and give it the job of making those dreams a reality.

But money isn't just going to show up at your door to whisk you away and spoil you with all your heart's desires. Just like the hottie of your dreams isn't going to search for you while you hunker down inside your house binging on Moose Tracks ice cream and *Fixer Upper* reruns. In order to receive, you have to give. And if you abuse it and squander your money on daily lattes, lottery tickets, or random items that get tossed in the cart during Target runs, it won't be there to give you the things or experiences you most desire. Your money wants to have a purpose in your life, and money dates help you get clear on what that purpose is.

If you want your money to be there for you and help you create a swoon-worthy life, you have to make your money a priority and set aside time to tend to your money relationship. Most women don't take time to regularly tend to their finances because they have complicated feelings about money. They feel overwhelmed, anxious, and confused by all things money.

So, they avoid dealing with their finances, bury their heads in the sand, and wish upon a star that they'll win the lottery or receive a surprise inheritance check in the mail that will solve all their money problems. When money feels "hard to get" or like it's ghosting you when you need it most, the last thing you want to do is take the time to look through your finances and see what's *really* going on. But avoiding problems doesn't solve them. It just makes them bigger and scarier.

Tending to your finances doesn't have to feel like a total borefest or a complete drag though. When you treat your money like a romantic partner, like a dreamy crush you're so hot for, and schedule fun money dates to catch up with your money and see what it's been up to, you start thinking, feeling, and behaving differently with your money. After a while, tending to your finances starts to feel like one, big, guilty pleasure that you look forward to.

Personifying your money, giving it a personality, and imagining that it has feelings, hopes, and dreams (just like you) takes the confusion and overwhelm out of your money relationship and replaces it with curiosity, intrigue, and confidence. The more time you spend with your money, the better you'll get to know it. Then you'll take care of it better, and you'll make more of it. Scheduling regular money dates is the key to having a happy, healthy relationship with money and starting a money love affair that will last a lifetime. Money dates need to be scheduled, or they won't happen. Ideally, you'll carve out an hour every week for a money date. Consistency is key; don't make excuses and stand your money up!

MONEY TRUTH: When you start loving money, it starts loving you back and wants to be around you ALL the time to fill your life with joy, pleasure, and financial freedom.

Every good relationship takes effort, and your relationship with money is no different. Ready to rekindle your relationship with money and add some spice to your financial life? Great! The next step is to pick which type of money date you want to start with!

There are 4 different types of first money dates:

1. The Blind Date

Just as I shared in my own story, the blind money date can be a little scary and intimidating, but thrilling and exciting at the same time! You just don't know what you're going to get or how it will go. How suspenseful! The "blind" money date is basically the first time you sit down and take a good look at what's really happening with your finances. Cold feet are normal with this type of money date because you might be fearing the worst. What if you discover your debt is way more than you thought? What if you find out that someone's stolen your credit card number and ruined your credit score?

Fearing the worst will likely make you want to skip out on the blind money date before it even begins, but what if you learn that there's more money in your account than you suspected? What if you discover that your money has been hard at work earning interest for you? This blind money date might be the start of a lifelong love affair after all!

2. Set Up by a Friend

Your friend knows money, likes it, trusts it, and is good with it. She recommends a financial advisor, financial therapist, coach, banker, or money expert to help you improve your money relationship and financial life. Jackpot! Based on her recommendation, you schedule a consultation with the financial professional she suggested. You'll likely feel positive and optimistic about this money date because there's less risk involved. You trust your friend's opinion and feel confident the professional she recommended is trustworthy. Getting help from a financial professional is a great way to start a new, sexy relationship with money! Who knows? Maybe you'll ask the friend who set you up to stand by you when you say "I do" to your money and get filthy rich!

3. Love at First Sight

You just got a windfall of money through an inheritance, a winning lottery ticket, a killer launch, the sale of a house, an advance on your book, or a big investor. Let it rain money! Woohoo! How amazing and crush-worthy! Money is finally here! It's like all of your problems just got solved. You get swept up in the romance of it all. You are totally swooning over all your beautiful money. It's like love at first sight!

It's easy to get carried away in the heat of the moment, but the best thing to do is schedule a money date to make concrete plans about what you'll do with the money. Reflect on the best use for that money. Should it go toward paying off debt? A down payment on a house? Saved in an emergency fund? Fund a dream vacation? Use this money date to research and soul search. Then, decide what you'll do with the cash.

4. Friends First

This type of dating is all about taking it nice and slow with your money. You already know your money, but you start looking at it differently. You want to get to know your finances better and know yourself better, too. You and your money hang out together often. You have fun and chill together. You daydream about everything you could do together in the future, but there's zero pressure. Being friends with money first gives you time and space to think back to previous relationships with money. What worked? What didn't? What can you do better this time around to make this relationship last? You love talking with your money and exploring where your hopes and dreams line up with what money can do for you.

The safety of this friendship lets you ask some tough money questions like, "What can you bring to my life and how can you help me become the best version of myself?" Slow and steady is the name of the game as you let the love build organically and naturally. This approach can lead to a passion-filled, long-lasting relationship with money. It's the kind of relationship where you see money as a friend and not an enemy. You feel confident in your financial decisions and in control of how much you're spending. You know where all your money is going.

Chapter 8

First Date Jitters

First dates can be so awkward. You agonize over what to wear, changing your outfit five times before settling on one that's not too dressy, but not too casual. You spend two hours blowing out your hair and getting your cat eyeliner perfect. Butterflies swirl around in your belly as you wonder what the evening will be like. Will you say something stupid? Will the date lead to wedding bells or flop like a low-budget horror film? What if you kiss? OMG! What if you have bad breath? AHHH!

You might be feeling just as overwhelmed about having your first date with your money. Jitters are common at the start of any new relationship. When you start dating someone new, you feel the rush of excitement and possibility. "Could this be the ONE?" But you also have a lot of doubts. "What if this relationship crashes and burns like all the others? What if all my hopes and dreams for this relationship fall apart? What if I invest a boatload of time and energy into this relationship and it's still not what I want?" The "what-ifs" can drive you mad!

If you're feeling these new relationship jitters with your money, you're not alone. Maybe you haven't always been a "good girlfriend" in previous money relationships. One minute, you'd be telling your money how much you love it and how you always want it to be around. The next, you'd betray your money with a shopping spree at Macy's.

In past money relationships, you'd feel like everything was going along great. Your money was a hottie, and you were sharing fun, flirty times together, but then you'd find yourself waking up to a maxed-out credit card after a night out with the girls. It's all a blur. What *happened* last night?

Maybe your past money relationships were filled with suspicion. "Where the hell is my money going?" It's never fun to worry about cheating, and you never again want to find yourself snooping through bank statements and boxes of receipts to track down where your money has been. And, OMG, let's not talk about all the messy breakups you've had with money in the past. They were probably pretty messy and unpleasant. So over it!

But that's why you're here. You're ready to change all that. You're ready to be a "good girlfriend" to your money and build a new money relationship that will last—without all the money drama, cheating, or credit card one-night stands. You want a steamy love affair with your money, a relationship built on honesty and trust, and a partnership that can weather any storm.

It's not all your fault that you weren't a good girlfriend to your money in the past. You probably didn't have a money fairy godmother giving you money advice or waving her magic wand so all your financial dreams could come true. That's what I'm here for. To be your money fairy godmother, your legit money therapist, a trusted guide to show you how to create a fairytale love story with your money! The first step is to start dating your money by planning some money dates.

First, I want to point out that getting back in the dating game isn't always easy, and you might be wondering what a money date looks like exactly. Well, there are about a million things you could do with money to make for a sexy, flirty money date! To help you come up with some date ideas of your own, here are some tips:

- Brainstorm as many date ideas as you can. (I've listed several ideas below to help you get started.) Even if they sound weird. Do a massive brain dump. Write it all down on paper, and sort through it later.
- Be creative! Have fun with the process. A sense of humor goes a long way.
- Review all your ideas positively. Don't criticize your ideas or yourself.
- Circle your favorite ideas and do them!

To give you an idea of how fun money dates can be, here are seven money date ideas you could go on right now:

1. Netflix & Chill

Grab the popcorn. Pull on those sweatpants. Snuggle up on the couch with a hot cup of coffee and turn on Netflix. Action adventure? Romantic comedy? Nope. Tonight is all about...money documentaries! Check out *Money Explained*, *The Minimalists: Less is More*, or *Saving Capitalism*. When it's over, have some juicy convos about what you learned, either with a buddy or in your journal. How might those lessons apply to you? What were some sweet takeaways you can apply to your money relationship?

2. Night Out on the Town
Tonight's the night to whip out the mini skirt and slip on the stilettos! Get ready for pink champagne, bottle service, fine dining, and a Broadway play! Well, kinda. Before your hot night out with money, you've got some planning to do. Look up the price for each of those things and add it all up. How much does it cost for a glitzy night out on the town? Challenge yourself to get the same experience at one-third of the cost. Have cocktail hour at home with a bottle of Tisdale Pinot Noir ($5, baby!) and chips with salsa. (Still wear the stilettos.) Hit up the half-priced sushi night and indulge in the $8 slice of cheesecake from the best bakery in town. Substitute the Broadway show with the "pay-what-you-wish" comedy club. Then roll around in all the money you saved when you get home (and slip out of that mini skirt). In this case, it's good to be a "cheap date."

3. Girl's Night
Yoga pants. Pizza with extra cheese. Wine. Lots of wine. '80s pop music streaming in the background and girl talk. Gather around with your favorite ladies or hop on a Zoom call. Tonight is for dishing about money. What do you love about it? Hate about it? What about money drives you crazy? What makes you want more money? Sends you into a frenzy? What are your hopes, dreams, and fears about money? Tell all! Leave nothing out! Just wait until you hear what your girls have to say about it.

4. Podcast Date

Pretend for a moment that your money is the object of your affection and you're completely obsessed with it. I don't mean obsessed in a "I need more and more money" sort of way, but rather in an "OMG, my money is the bomb dot com, and I adore it so much" sort of way. Because you're crushing so hard on your money, you want to know as much about it as you possibly can. Every. Single. Detail. One of the easiest (and most pleasurable) ways to learn more about money is to listen to podcasts! There are a gazillion podcasts about money where you can learn about everything from investing to budgeting to caring for your financial health.

Here are a few money podcasts you might swoon over:

1. *Money You Should Ask* with Bob Wheeler (It was SO fun to be a guest on this show!)
2. *The Micro Empires Podcast* with Jennifer Grimson (I adore Jennifer and was delighted to be a guest on her show, too!)
3 *Clever Girl Finance Podcast* with Bola Sokunbi
4. *Financial Grownup Podcast* with Bobbie Rebell
5. *The Mental Health & Wealth Podcast* with Melanie Lockert (I was a guest on this show, too!)
6. *Popcorn Finance Podcast* with Chris Browning
7. *The Breadwinners Podcast* with Jennifer Owens and Rachel Ellison
8. *Bigger Pockets Podcast* with Brandon Turner
9. *Ladies Get Paid Podcast* with Claire Wasserman
10. *Paychecks and Balances Podcast* with Rich Jones
11. *Marriage, Kids, and Money Podcast* with Andy Hill

For this money date, pick one (or several!) of these podcasts and devour the episodes as if they were a decadent slice of double-cream cheesecake dripping with caramel sauce. Soak up all the information, tips, and financial advice like it's a Double Stuf Oreo soaking up milk. Write down some of your favorite takeaways from each episode and make a plan for how you'll apply it to your financial life. Get completely obsessed with learning all about your money. Wanna really crank up the heat on your money love affair? Leave a glowing review of any of the shows you adore. Good things come to those who do good.

5. A Trip Down Memory Lane

Pull out the family photo album. It's time to reminisce! Flip through the pages and think back to your first money memories. How did your parents handle money? What did they teach you about it? Do you think those lessons serve you well today? Remember when you lost your money virginity (you know, your first experience with money). What was that like for you? Positive? Negative? Reflect on your previous relationships with money at various stages in your life. How do those memories affect how you feel about money now?

For example, I had my first experience with money when I was five years old. I sold magazines for the kindergarten fundraiser, and my prize was to scoop nickels out of a bucket and keep whatever I could grab. My tiny hand held on to as many nickels as it could, and I celebrated as I dumped them into a plastic bag, excited to have my own money to buy the Lisa Frank stationary set I'd had my eyes on.

My celebration was premature. After counting the nickels, I realized I didn't have enough for the stationary set. I was shattered. That experience led me to believe that opportunities to make money are scarce, and when one comes along, you have to grab and fight for as much money as you can get. If you don't, you'll be left wanting.

6. Money Threesome

Sexy lingerie. Marvin Gaye singing "Let's Get It On." All the lights dimmed. This date is for passion, heat, and a threesome. You. Money. AND your partner. It can be a romantic partner, a BFF, or a business partner. (Maybe rethink the lingerie if it's business-related.) Once the mood is set, it's time to share your wildest fantasies...about what you'd do if you had all the money you want. Digging down into the depths of desire, reveal all the hot details about where you'd go, what you'd want to experience or buy, how you'd want to feel, what clothes you'd wear, and who you'd hang out with. Now bring it to life. Make a plan and a promise to attract your desires to create the life you want.

7. Coffee Date

Where: Starbucks. Dunkin Donuts. Or that super cute coffee shop down the street. When: Anytime you want coffee (so, like, *any time*). What: Savoring a hot vanilla latte and catching up with your money to see what it's been up to all week. Serious people might call it budgeting or balancing the checkbook. We call it "quality time."

Once you've decided what you want to do with your money, the only thing left to do is **schedule** your dates! If it ain't scheduled, it ain't happenin'. And if money dates don't happen, you'll have a number of problems, and money will be at the top of the list! It's time to get down to business and make your money a priority by locking down money dates on your calendar and keeping them just like you would a doctor's appointment, an interview with Oprah, or a hair appointment with the stylist who has a year-long waitlist. No excuses. No bailing on your money. Nothing but quality time with your money!

Add even more spice to your money relationship by sharing your money dates with friends. Go ahead and change your status to "in a relationship." Get your phone ready to take a ton of selfies. Just like with any new relationship, you'll want the world to know how much fun you're having on these money dates. Share photos, dish all the drama from your dates, and swoon over your latest financial crush on social media. Post a comment on Instagram with the caption, "Dreaming and making plans with my money about all the cool things we'll do over the next five years! #moneydate." One of the best ways to love up your money is to brag about how awesome it is. You just might inspire others to start having money dates too. Start a trend!

Whatever money date you plan, make sure it's fun and enjoyable—something to look forward to. You might be thinking that this is easier said than done, especially if you've had negative experiences with money in the past. Old money baggage can certainly interfere with getting this new money relationship off to a good start.

Chapter 9

Old Money Baggage

We've all had them: those relationships that completely tanked and left you feeling like you've just been hit by a Mack truck. Those devastating, epic-fail relationships can leave you heartbroken and jaded. You start to think that everyone sucks and you'll never find love. Why even bother? *Cue the violins.*

When a relationship goes tragically wrong, it's hard to open yourself up to someone new and trust that things might be different this time. It can be a challenge to not punish your new love interest for the other jerk's mistakes. If you've had some not-so-hot experiences with money in the past—like racking up huge amounts of debt, paying bills late, living paycheck-to-paycheck, or having absolutely no idea how much you're making or spending—you've probably got some money relationship baggage.

"What's money relationship baggage look like?" you ask. It looks like FEAR and made-up stories you tell yourself about money that feel like facts but are really just a bunch of bull crap. Here are some common fears:

- You'll have to give something up in exchange for your money, like time with loved ones, leisure or travel time, or self-care to hustle and grind at work.
- You'll lose something, or someone, precious to you if you have more money, like fearing your partner will leave you if you get "too successful, famous, or rich" or that you'll lose friends because they'll see you as a "rich bitch" who they can no longer relate to.
- You won't actually be able to change your financial situation, which would make you feel like a big, fat failure.
- People will try to take advantage of you if you have a lot of money, and you'll never be able to really trust anyone again.
- You'll resort to shady ways of making money; cheat people so you can get ahead; and become a terrible, horrible, no-good, very bad person just to get rich.

Sound familiar? Now, we want to nip that baggage in the bud so you don't bring it into this new relationship with your money and sabotage the whole thing. It's no small feat to shift your beliefs about money. It takes time and practice, but this book will show you how to create a head-over-heels, fairytale love story with your money. I'm getting ahead of myself though. Before you can give your money relationship a makeover, you need to examine what the relationship looks like right now.

Chapter 10

Start Where You're At

No two people look exactly alike, nor do any two relationships look alike. We all have different life experiences, upbringings, perspectives, and challenges. As such, our financial lives all start at different points. Some people are born into wealthy families and are offered numerous advantages that others could only dream of. Discrimination, racism, sexism, ableism, ageism, and oppression are factors that can significantly affect financial stability and success.

For example, women face unique financial challenges that men often don't face. Men are still paid higher wages than women, even when they do the exact same job. On average, women tend to live about ten years longer than men. As such, they need more money in their retirement years to support themselves for the rest of their days. Yet, women are often the ones who take more time away from paid work to raise children or care for aging parents. Not to mention, goods and services are priced higher for women than men, costing women more in living expenses. (Why is a man's haircut $20 and a woman's $45?) It's not an equal playing field. In the money game, there are unfair advantages and raw deals. Social issues and injustices don't necessarily determine your financial future, but they can definitely affect the trajectory of your financial life.

I'll use myself as an example here. My life started out, well, UNwealthy. My mother was young, single, and unprepared for parenthood. She wanted to live her life, not take care of the many demands of an infant. She often left me in the care of my grandparents: good, old-fashioned, blue-collar folks from the Midwest who had little to nothing but would give you the shirt off their backs.

I grew up in an environment that taught me I had to hustle and grind to get ahead. It wasn't polite to talk about money; you should wait to be offered the raise instead of asking for it; working two or three jobs was totally normal. Those messages stuck with me for a long time and eventually led to the ugly financial crisis that completely rocked my world.

That financial disaster was a wake-up call, and it gave me a burning desire for a better life. I wanted to have money to travel and experience new things. I wanted to feel confident and in control of my finances. I wanted to have financial power so I could change the world for the better and have a big impact. I didn't want to struggle like my grandparents, and I didn't want to be kept from living my dreams because I couldn't afford them.

I fantasized about my money sweeping me off my feet and saving me from a life of struggle. But I never really thought it would ever happen to me. It wasn't until I took a hard look at what my money relationship was like in that moment; realizing it wasn't the relationship I wanted for myself; and envisioning, in great detail, the fairytale love story I wanted to have with my money.

Clarity = Power. You gotta know what you want before you'll get it. You gotta see it in your mind, feel it in your soul, and have a burning desire for it. You may not be able to control the world, end all injustices, and level the money playing field, but you are the author of your own life story. You get to decide how you'll think, feel, and behave with your money. You get to decide what kind of relationship you'll have with money. You get to determine how much money you'll make and how you'll go about earning that money. You get to create your own fairytale love story with your money!

But first, you need to take a teensy bit of time and describe what your money relationship looks like right now. No judgment. No beating yourself up because your money relationship looks worse than a thrown-up hairball. Wherever you are right now is where you're supposed to be, and clearly identifying what turns you off about your current money relationship will help you discover what you want to change.

Ask yourself the following questions and jot down your answers:

1. What's going well in your money relationship?
2. What's not going well?
3. How do you feel when you think about money?
4. What does it feel like when you tend to your finances?
5. On a scale of 1-10 (1 = not at all, 10 = completely), how confident are you in your financial decisions?

6. On a scale of 1-10 (1 = not at all, 10 = completely), how confident are you in your ability to earn as much money as you want?
7. What's one word that describes the feeling you get when you think about the amount of debt you have?
8. True or False: "I trust my money to be there when I need it."
9. Which celebrity couple best represents your current relationship with money?
    A. Michael J. Fox & Tracey Pollan: complete marital bliss for over three decades!
    B. Brad Pitt & Jennifer Aniston: seemed like love at first sight but took a sharp turn toward Drama-town!
    C. Britney Spears & Jason Alexander: an impulsive, hot mess marriage that only lasted fifty-five hours!

10. What happens when you try to talk to your partner/clients/friends/family about money?

    A. Talk about money? Um, that's not happening.
    B. I'm a pro! All my money convos are calm and productive.
    C. I usually end up ugly crying and then hiding under the covers.

Great job, love! Now you've got a good sense of where your money relationship is. This will help you to know what you want to keep doing in this new money relationship and what you want to do differently.

I'm sure you're ready to fall in love for keeps with your money and live happily ever after in money marriage bliss. So, what separates long-lasting relationships from short-lived ones? What will it take for your money to want to stick around until death do you part? That's what we'll dive into next. But first, your assignment.

Money Therapy Assignment

Schedule Your Money Dates

Grab your planner and your favorite colored pens. Take a look at your schedule for this week and find a one-hour block of time that's open. Book a money date and write it in pen so you don't flake out! Decide which sexy, flirty money date you'd like to have. Maybe your date will be Netflix and chill—a night of cozy pj's, popcorn, and binging on money documentaries that will boost your financial knowledge. Or maybe you'll go for a low-key coffee date. You could even dream up your own fun, flirty money date idea!

Once you book your money date, keep it! No canceling. No excuses. Don't leave your money hanging. Treat your money date like a reservation at the hottest new restaurant in town or a backstage pass to a Taylor Swift concert. Do not bail on your money! Commit to spending quality time with your money.

Money Therapy
Assignment

PART III: FALLING IN LOVE FOR KEEPS

Chapter 11

Falling in Love for Keeps

Have you ever noticed how a couple in love seems adorable and endearing when you're in a happy relationship and downright annoying when you're single? When you're content in your own life, it's easy to be happy for other people's good fortune. But when someone else has what you deeply want for yourself, the green-eyed, envy monster rears its ugly head and hijacks all the good vibes.

It feels like cat puke when you see other people enjoying the success you want for yourself. This applies to all types of success: successful relationships, careers, parenting, and finances. When you start comparing yourself and your situation to other people, self-critical questions start popping up like weeds in a garden:

"What do they got that I don't got?"

"What am I doing wrong?"

"How is it that I'm working my tail off and still not seeing the results I want?"

"Why does it look so easy for them and so hard for me?"

The answers are unclear and feel so far out of reach. Reaching your financial goals seems so far out of reach, too. How many times have you listened to podcasts that feature multi-millionaires telling the story of how they became rich by only working four hours a week? Or watched someone glide into the driver's seat of the BMW you've been wanting for years? Or saw pictures on Instagram of friends relaxing on the beach or spending a month sightseeing in Europe? Everywhere you look, it seems like everyone but you has a strong, sexy relationship with their money, and while their glamorous money relationship might just be the highlight reel, you admire it...and you want it for yourself.

What makes those money relationships so great? How can you create a money relationship that looks and feels like the ones you see other people experiencing? If you've never experienced a happy money relationship before, it's hard to know what to look for. If you don't know what to look for, you won't know when you have it. If you don't know when you have a happy money relationship, you'll keep hustling to create it, spinning your wheels and feeling defeated in the process.

I've worked with *a lot* of couples, and because of my experience as a therapist, it's easy for me to tell if a couple is happy or not, whether I meet them inside or outside of the therapy office. There are certain traits that successful relationships possess, and these same traits apply to successful money relationships as well.

Here are the ten key features of happy relationships (both romantically & financially):

1. Companionship & Friendship

Hello, money dates! You want to be friends with your money, spend time together, and have fun together. Love up on each other on the regular by scheduling (and showing up for) weekly money dates.

2. Communicate Softly

Criticism comes up in all relationships, and you might find yourself being critical of your money, like when you find out your salary is significantly less than your dude counterpart or you get socked with a late payment fee. You don't want to unleash your temper on your money. So, you gotta start soft and talk through it gently. In literal terms, this means being mindful of the thoughts you have about your financial situation and choosing non-judgment and patience over frustration and anger.

3. Let Your Partner Influence You

People in happy money relationships allow their money to influence their decisions rather than just doing whatever they want and expecting their money to be at their beck and call. This means working with a spending plan (a.k.a. budget) and living within your means.

4. Using Tools for Solving Conflict

There are some handy-dandy money management tools you'll learn about in part six. Using those tools consistently will help prevent conflict and financial problems from arising. Plus, good financial tools make tending to your finances feel fun and flirty instead of boring and overwhelming.

5. Tolerating Faults

Everyone makes mistakes and messes up from time to time. You might take a misstep that you're not happy about. Your money might not always be there for you in the exact way you want. Taking the bad with the good is an important part of having a happy relationship.

6. Honoring Each Other's Dreams

You have big dreams about what you'll do with your money, and your money wants to make them come to life. If your money could talk, it would tell you that it doesn't want you slaving away at a job you hate for the sake of earning a steady paycheck. Your money's dream for you is to do work you love and use the money you earn from that work to live your best life. Honoring each other's dreams is a recipe for happiness!

7. Knowing Each Other's Worlds Intimately

At all times, you want to be actively involved with your money and always aware of what's going on with it. Your spending plan helps you to stay intimately connected with your money, and it helps your money know what financial goals you're working on together at any given time.

8. Turn Toward Each Other Instead of Away

When the going gets tough, happy couples don't run away from each other. They run toward one another. When you face a financial struggle or crisis, you want to spend even more time with your money to figure things out instead of avoiding it and burying your head in the sand, hoping all the money problems will disappear. (They won't.)

9. Share Power & Tasks

Happy couples share decision-making power and responsibilities. The burdens don't fall on just one person in the relationship. The same goes for your money relationship. While you're busy earning an income, your money is busy earning interest or paying an accountant to help you minimize your tax liability. It's a team effort.

10. Differentiation Exists

Differentiation is the balance between sharing a life together with someone and having an independent life of your own. It's something that all couples are constantly working toward. You and your money have to work toward differentiation, too. You want to know all about your money, but you don't want to be so obsessed with it that it rules your life. It's about keeping the balance between loving your money while also loving all the other things in your life.

Chapter 12

Money Relationship Myths

Now that you know what a happy, healthy relationship with money looks like and the importance of treating your money relationship like a romantic one, we need to talk about some money relationship myths that can sabotage living happily ever after with your money.

MYTH #1: You can have it all.
This money relationship myth is half true. You can have it all, *just not all at the same time.* I'm sure you have big dreams for what you and your money will do together and all the things your money will bring to your life. That's cool. But if you think that your money is going to bring you the dream house, the boat, the million-dollar investment portfolio, the month-long vacation to Greece, and pay off all your student loans in the same year, you really are dreaming.

You don't want to set up your money relationship to fail. So, you need to have realistic expectations. You can have all the things on your bucket list . . . eventually. Just don't be like Veruca Salt in *Charlie and the Chocolate Factory* when she demands a golden goose, another pony, and the whole world NOW!

MYTH #2: Your money will wait forever to be a priority in your life.

We've already established that your money needs your time and attention. Having weekly money dates is how you consistently devote time and attention to your money. If you don't make your money a priority, it isn't going to wait around for your attention. It's gonna jet and go find someone else who will meet its needs.

It's just like in *Friends* when Ross professed his love for Rachel, but she dismissed him and said she just wanted to be friends. Ross had no choice but to move on. So, he started dating Emily, which made Rachel super jealous and filled with regret for missing her chance with Ross. Your money is professing its love for you whenever it's around. Don't make the mistake of assuming it's gonna wait for you to notice it and love it back.

MYTH #3: The grass is greener. The bank accounts are bigger.

Couples get into deep trouble when they look at other people's relationships and make a comparison. "Her husband cooks dinner EVERY night while my husband plays video games on his phone! Why can't my hubby be more like that?"

"Jess and her wife are always taking trips together and going on romantic adventures, but I haven't had a getaway with my wife since we got married. What gives?" You might do this very same thing with money relationships.

"OMG, she drives the Land Rover I've always wanted! I wanna do what she does so I can have what she has!"

"She's been at her job for five years and makes $100,000 while I've been hustling for ten years and only make $70,000. This sucks! What am I doing wrong?"

Looks can be deceiving. The grass isn't always greener, even if it appears that way. You don't know what that woman had to do for that Land Rover. Maybe it was something totally shitty or something you would never want to do yourself. Or maybe she lays awake at night worrying about how to pay that massive car payment.

That $100,000 a year she's making? What she's not telling you is that she's at her boss's beck and call, works ninety-hour weeks, and is $50,000 in debt. Do you still want what she's got? Keep your eyes on your own paper. I mean, relationship. I mean, money.

Chapter 13

Codependency

The fourth (and final) myth that can sabotage your money relationship is a doozy, so it deserves some deeper conversation.

MYTH #4: The money relationship is all about you and what money can do for you. OR the money relationship is all about what you can do for money.

Why do you think people get married? Do you think that when someone dreams about meeting their soulmate and starting a life with that person they make a mental laundry list of all the things they can do to make their honey happy or how they can go out of their way on a daily basis to make their spouse's life easier? Um, no.

Sure, most people want relationships to be mutually beneficial, but the focus usually isn't on how to make the other person feel constantly loved and adored. Humans are sort of inherently self-centered. Our survival instincts make us that way. So, when it comes to love, we all tend to focus on what we can *get* from our mate, not what we can *give*. That leads to this idea that the relationship is all about you and that your sweetie should be going out of their way to make you happy. If they don't? Well, there's gonna be words.

A lot of couples buy into this myth, and I can tell you from my experience sitting in hundreds of couple's therapy sessions that extreme individualism doesn't make for a good relationship. In fact, when one person is stuck in the role of taker and the other is stuck in the role of giver, the relationship becomes **codependent**.

For any relationship to be happy and healthy, it takes teamwork, compromise, caring, and thoughtfulness. The relationship needs to be equitable: give *and* take. When it comes to your money, are you all up in its business, like, "When are you going to get me the new selection of Lululemon yoga clothes I've been eyeing up?" Are you all irritated and annoyed with your cash, like, "Why can't you help out more and pay off this credit card already? It's been five years!"

If you answered "yes," then you're the *dependent* in the money relationship: the *taker*. When you're always "gimme more, gimme more" to your money, it gets sad and feels unappreciated, and that makes your money not want to do jack shit for you. I mean, if your money made everything about what it could get from you without giving anything in return, would you be interested in doing it any favors? Hellz to the no.

You might swing the other way though. You might be the *enabler* in the money relationship: the *giver*. Do you find yourself dragging your butt to a corporate job you hate, giving away your precious time and energy, just to keep a steady paycheck and benefits? Are you constantly hustling and grinding, working harder and harder, giving more and more at work, just to prove you're worthy of the salary you're paid? Are you taking on nightmare clients who make constant demands because you feel desperate for cash?

Whenever you're relying on your money to meet all your psychological, emotional, and physical needs (i.e. make you blissfully happy all the time), or you're devoting all your time and energy to making money in ways that aren't fulfilling, you're in a codependent relationship with money.

Codependency can cause some major money relationship problems:

- It makes it harder to make financial decisions.
- It brings up complicated feelings about money.
- It makes it more difficult to talk about money.
- It makes you value the approval of others more than valuing yourself.
- It can create a lack of trust in yourself and your ability to earn money.
- It can increase fear and anxiety about money.
- It can keep you stuck in habits that aren't serving you well.

I wasn't aware of it at the time, but I found myself in a codependent relationship with money, and it almost cost me my entrepreneurial dreams. Before I started my counseling practice, I was in search of a job. My husband and I had just moved from Colorado to Pennsylvania, and I was waiting around for my clinical license to transfer from state to state.

I knew I wanted to start my own business eventually, but I was five months pregnant, bored out of my mind, and wanted to get back to work. Besides, I needed to make some money for my growing family. We lived in a rural area, so jobs in my field were slim pickings. Most of them paid crappy hourly wages, wanted me to be on call, and demanded intense work hours.

But there was one job posting that caught my eye: temporary professor of social work at the local college. At that time in my life, this was my dream job, and now it was staring me in the face! I always had a passion for teaching, and I saw this as my chance to finally do it. It was perfect. The temporary position would give me work until I had the baby, and it offered good pay and benefits.

I immediately applied and waited. And waited. And waited. Crickets. When I couldn't wait any longer and no other jobs popped up, I decided to start my private practice and make a job for myself. I devoted my life to growing my mental health practice and, later, started a second business doing Money Therapy. Life was busy, and my career was moving forward.

I didn't really think about that teaching position again until six years later when I got a call from the college asking me if I wanted to be a temporary professor of social work for the next three semesters. I couldn't believe it. My dream job was handed to me on a silver platter. No application needed, and no interview required. The job was mine if I wanted it. I snatched it up.

It was just as I thought it would be. I loved teaching, the students, and academia. Even more so, I loved the money and knowing exactly how much I'd make each week! I loved the 401(k) and the dental and vision insurance, things I didn't have as a self-employed entrepreneur.

I became dependent on those benefits, and I didn't want to lose them ever. I started plotting and planning for how I could turn that temporary position into a permanent gig so I could keep all that money and benefits forever. I became obsessed with doing whatever it took for that kind of financial stability. I even applied to a doctorate program and planned on investing $30,000 and three years of my life so I would have the credentials to get a permanent position as a professor.

While I was giving my all in exchange for financial predictability, I was no longer nurturing my online Money Therapy business. It was put to the side to collect dust, and I missed it. I started thinking about all the plans I had for growing my business and helping women take a more active role in their finances. I truly wanted to change women's lives for the better.

While working in that temporary position, I started getting frustrated with the bureaucratic bullshit that comes with working in a large organization and started remembering why I became my own boss in the first place. This led to some deep soul-searching, and I realized the codependent relationship I'd created with money wasn't healthy. It was motivating me to make decisions that didn't make me happy. I had to choose. Did I want to devote my time and energy to becoming a tenure-track professor with a steady paycheck and full benefits but deal with red tape and corporate crap? Or did I want to devote my time and energy to growing my Money Therapy business, navigating variable pay, but doing the work I love and making a greater impact in the world?

I'm here with you now, so you know what I chose. But it wasn't an easy decision. The money and benefits in that other job were very tempting, and I almost got caught up in it. But I knew that if my money love affair was going to last, the relationship had to be mutually beneficial, not codependent.

So, how about you? Are you ready to break out of these money relationship myths for good? Are you ready to finally change your money relationship for the better? If you're raising your hand, you need to know this: All-or-nothing thinking is what makes you buy into these myths. Believing you can have it all or telling yourself that you're completely broke is all-or-nothing thinking. It's black *or* white. It's this *or* that. But in reality, we live in the gray zone. That's where balance exists, and hanging out in the middle of two extremes is where you want to be.

The truth is that you can have some things now and some things later. A little of this and a little of that. If you're thinking in extremes, like thinking that in order to always have health insurance, you can never be self-employed, then you're going to feel really, really bad. And you'll likely create a codependent relationship with your money.

All-or-nothing thinking is a cognitive distortion—an automatic, irrational thought. Did you catch that? It's an *irrational* way of thinking. Keep reading to learn more about how this affects your money relationship.

Chapter 14

Cognitive Distortions

Absolutely everyone experiences cognitive distortions. I spend a lot of time teaching my therapy clients about cognitive distortions, and we practice identifying irrational thoughts on an ongoing basis because whenever you're experiencing a cognitive distortion, you feel awful.

In order to feel good (and behave better), you have to go through this process:

- Notice the thought that's making you feel bad (about money, work, relationships, etc.).
- Identify the type of cognitive distortion you're experiencing.
- Challenge the irrational thought.
- Form a healthier thought that makes you feel better.

- Do a happy dance that you took control of your thoughts and protected your money relationship. (Optional, but highly encouraged.)

There are ten types of cognitive distortions, and this nifty cheat sheet shows you what each of them looks like:

TYPE OF COGNITIVE DISTORTION	EXAMPLE RELATED TO THE MONEY RELATIONSHIP
1. All-or-Nothing Thinking: You see things in black-or-white categories. If your performance falls short of perfect, you see yourself as a total failure.	"I didn't make my car payment on time this month. I'm never going to get my financial shit together and pay bills on time."
2. Overgeneralization: You see a single negative event as a never-ending pattern of defeat.	"I overdrafted my bank account today, which must mean that I'm terrible with money."
3. Mental Filter: You pick out a single negative detail and dwell on it exclusively so that your vision of all reality becomes darkened, like the drop of ink that colors the entire beaker of water.	"I have SO much credit card debt! My financial situation is a complete mess because of all these damn credit cards! Credit cards are the bane of my existence!"

4. Disqualifying the Positive: You reject positive experiences by insisting they "don't count" for some reason or another. In this way, you can maintain a negative belief that is contradicted by your everyday experiences.

"So what if I paid off my car loan? That's nothing. I still have all these student loans hanging over my head."

5. Jumping to Conclusions: You make a negative interpretation even though there are no definite facts that convincingly support your conclusion.
   1. *Mind Reading:* You arbitrarily conclude that someone is reacting negatively to you, and you don't bother to check this out.
   2. *The Fortune Teller Error:* You anticipate that things will turn out badly and you feel convinced that your prediction is an already-established fact (self-fulfilling prophecy).

"I just know my boss is going to reject my request for a pay raise. There's no point in even asking for one."

"There's no way I'll ever become a millionaire. It's completely impossible, a total pipe dream."

6. Magnification (Catastrophizing or Minimization): You exaggerate the importance of things (such as your goof-up or someone else's achievement), or you inappropriately shrink things until they appear tiny (your own desirable qualities or someone else's imperfections). This is also called the "binocular trick."

"OMG! I forgot to pay a bill on time, and now I'm getting whacked with a late fee! My credit is going to be ruined! I'll never get a loan again!"

"Sarah's crushing it financially. She's only forty years old and is getting ready to retire. I wish I could be more like her. She's got everything figured out."

7. Emotional Reasoning: You assume that your negative emotions necessarily reflect the way things really are: "I feel it; therefore, it must be true."

"I feel like I'm going to wake up one day and all my money will be gone. Therefore, I know for sure that I'm going to wake up one day to find an empty bank account and nothing to live on."

8. Should Statements: You try to motivate yourself with shoulds and shouldn'ts, as if you had to be whipped and punished before you could be expected to do anything. "Musts" and "oughts" are also used. The emotional consequence is guilt. When you direct should statements toward others, you feel anger, frustration, and resentment.

"I should be making more money by now. I should work harder and put in more hours to increase my income."

"My partner should be doing a better job controlling his spending. He's wrecking our budget."

"My financial advisor ought to choose better investments. Is he even looking at my accounts?"

9. Labeling and Mislabeling: This is an extreme form of overgeneralization. Instead of describing your error, you attach a negative label to yourself: "I'm a loser." When someone else's behavior rubs you the wrong way, you attach a negative label to him: "He's a complete jerk." Mislabeling involves describing an event with language that is highly critical and emotionally loaded.

"I'm so bad with money! I'm terrible with numbers and math and a total idiot when it comes to finances!"

"My hair stylist charges twice as much as Karen's. What a greedy bitch!"

10. Personalization: You see yourself as the cause of some negative external event, which you were not primarily responsible for.	"My wife is always so stressed out about money. It's all my fault because I don't earn enough."

*Adapted from *Feeling Good by* David. D. Burns, M.D.

Whenever you're experiencing a cognitive distortion, you're going to feel like chewed-up dog breakfast, and your money relationship is going to be sabotaged by distorted thinking and relationship myths.

So, whenever your mind starts gravitating toward extremes and you find words like "always" or "never" popping up in your money relationship, challenge the cognitive distortion and take on a more rational way of thinking. Your goal is to find the gray zone, the happy balance between the extremes. Then, apply it to your money relationship.

For example, the gray zone for me is to be self-employed so I can do the work I love and be my own boss while setting aside money from my earnings to buy my own health insurance and save for retirement. I get the joy of having my own business and the comfort of financial stability.

When you find the gray zone and live there with your money, the relationship becomes mutually beneficial. You give a little, and your money gives a little. You take a little, and your money takes a little. WIN-WIN. Your money is happy about the things you do for it, and you're happy about the things money does for you.

Money Therapy Assignment

Money Codependency Quiz: a tool to help you gain awareness about the status of your money relationship and nip codependency in the bud as soon as it creeps up.

Not quite sure if you're stuck in a codependent relationship with your money? Want to make sure that you address any unhealthy aspects in your money relationship right away so they don't get out of control? This quiz will help you check on the quality of your money relationship and alert you to anything that needs to be worked on.

Take a look at these twenty questions and answer them as honestly as you can.

QUESTION	YES	NO
Does thinking about money make you extremely unhappy?		
Have your money problems ever affected your reputation in a negative way?		

Have you ever had to cancel plans with someone because you couldn't afford it?

Has the fear of financial instability kept you in a job you hate?

Have you ever felt the need to set aside dreams you have for yourself because of money?

Do you tend to hang on to money for as long as possible? Hoarding it? Afraid to let it go?

Have you ever borrowed money in order to save someone else from problems that weren't your own?

Do you ever feel as though you spend more on other people than you do on yourself?		
Do you tend to use your money to care for the needs of others before you take care of your own?		
Do the struggles you have with money ever cause you to lose sleep at night?		
Do you ever get the feeling that hustling for more money might be destroying you?		
Do you feel bad about yourself because you're not making as much money as you want?		

Do you go above and beyond to the point of burnout to make sure your boss/clients/customers are happy?

Do you live in constant fear that money is going to ghost you?

Do you try to figure out what will make you the most money so that you can do those things?

Do you spend a great deal of time obsessing about money and how it affects your life?

Have you put your entrepreneurial dreams aside for a steady paycheck or benefits?

Do you ever feel as though you do things that don't feel good or right for money?

Do you ever manipulate other people in order to get ahead financially?

When someone is asking you to do something for them for free or is asking for money from you, do you have a hard time saying "no"?

Tally your responses. If you answered "yes" to more than eleven questions, you're in a codependent relationship with your money. If this is you, be sure to challenge the all-or-nothing thinking and start making your money relationship a win-win.

And if you're on the verge of a freak out, thinking, *Shit, I'm codependent,* take a deep breath. Instead of pulling your hair out, celebrate your newfound awareness. Realizing the ways you're thinking about money all wrong is the first step toward change. Just keep reading. Next, I'll show you how your thoughts, feelings, and behaviors related to money are all connected and what you can do to set them right.

PART IV: MONEY PSYCHOLOGY 101

Chapter 15

Using Your Mind as a Tool

The mind is a powerful money-making tool. The thing about tools though is that they're totally useless if you don't know what to do with them. If you haven't been taught how to use a power saw, chances are, you'll never use one. The saw would sit in the garage, collecting dust, and your vision for building a custom desk for your office would be just that: an idea and nothing more. When it comes to building your dream financial life, you're a tool—in a good way!

If I were to hand you my husband's toolbox, you'd find many gadgets to aid you in getting all kinds of projects done. You'd see hammers for driving nails, screwdrivers for screwing in screws, pliers for pulling, and wrenches for tightening and loosening. Your mind works in the same way as those tools in my husband's toolbox. Your mind is always there, at the ready, to get busy creating whatever you wish to create. Yet, if you don't know how to use your mind to create the money relationship and financial freedom you want, you'll be sitting around thinking instead of doing, making little to no progress on your money goals.

Think of it like this: Let's say you just had a money date cruising around the Home Goods store and found the perfect picture to hang in your home office. You go home, stroll into your office, and find just the right place for your new artwork. Now, this picture obviously isn't going to hang itself. So, you walk into the garage to look for some tools to get the job done quickly. You open the toolbox, and the first thing you see is a heavy-duty staple gun. You pull it out and take it into your office, ready to get that picture on the wall. But no matter how many times you try and how many staples you jam into the picture frame, it doesn't make the picture stay on the wall. You tried to achieve your goal one way, and it didn't work. Now, you have three choices:

- Keep trying to hang the picture with the staple gun.
- Try hanging the picture in a different way.
- Give up and say, "Screw the picture. I didn't like it anyway."

The definition of insanity is doing the same thing over and over while expecting different results, and you really, really love the picture. So, you decide to go with option two. This time, you grab a hammer and a nail. You drive the nail into the wall with the hammer and hang the picture on the nail. *Voila!* Mission accomplished! Good thing you tried a different method for achieving your goal because if you hadn't, your wall would be as bare as it was before or filled with random staples.

Now, relate this to your money. For most of your life, you've been thinking about money in one way—probably a way that isn't serving you that well (which is why you're reading this book). You've been trying to reach your financial goals by behaving in a certain way—a way that isn't working that great for you because you're still living paycheck-to-paycheck and stressing over how little money you have.

It's just like trying to hang the picture with a staple gun. You're trying and trying, but it's just not working. You have to think and behave differently with money. Pick a different tool to get the job done so you can accomplish the goal of having a love affair with your money and living financially free.

Sometimes, the way we have to go about solving a problem, or reaching a goal, seems counterintuitive. I mean, who came up with the idea of hammering a nail into the wall first and then hanging the little hook on the back of the picture onto that nail? It seems counterintuitive to not just drive the nail right through the picture to get it to stay on the wall, right?!

When you use your mind as a money-making tool, it can feel counterintuitive as well. When I describe *how* to use your mind in a way that will help you to make more money, open up more opportunities, make more connections, and achieve all your money dreams, you'll probably feel the pull of resistance. It's normal to feel skeptical. By being open to thinking in new ways, you'll be able to reach your financial goals in a fraction of the time and with way less stress and hassle.

As an entrepreneur, I've read a ton of books on business, taken many online courses, and hired some of the best business coaches to teach me how to build and grow my business. Almost everyone I've ever learned from has stressed the importance of having a profit. Everywhere I turned, people were telling me that I needed to set specific goals on a monthly basis for how much money I intended to make and map out the exact ways I would make that money. So, like a good girl, I did what I was told.

I mapped out exactly how much money I wanted to make each month and the number of sessions I needed to provide to reach my profit goals. Then, I fixated on those numbers. I swirled them around in my mind. I stressed over those numbers. And when I didn't get as many calls from clients as I had planned, didn't book as many sessions as I intended, and fell short of my profit goals, I felt like a complete failure who would never have the profitable business that I wanted. (Name that cognitive distortion! If you guessed labeling and all-or-nothing thinking, you get a prize!)

Every time I fell short of my profit plan, I fell into a state of depression and devoted my energy and attention to beating myself up over it instead of figuring out new ways to reach my profit goals. Once I stopped licking my wounds, I would start heaping pressure on myself to work harder and longer so I could get clients on my schedule and make money! I would think of different tactics to get more clients coming through the doors of my business; tactics that didn't feel great to me because they were slightly manipulative and a little too pushy for my taste, **but I had to meet my profit plan goals or else!!!**

I could feel myself losing my integrity before I even put those tactics into place, and it felt bad. Real bad. It felt like using a staple gun to hang a picture. Frustrating. Painful. Unproductive. And it created other problems to deal with. Like having to pry forty staples out of the wall and fill in all the holes, I could feel my sense of integrity and love for my work being sucked out of me by resorting to slimy methods to make more profits in my business.

I couldn't go on like that. I had to use my mind in a different way. I had to pick a different tool to make the money I wanted. I began to question the whole point of making a profit plan and realized that I was trying to control something that wasn't really within my power to influence or control. I was trying to control how many calls I got from clients, how many of those clients booked sessions with me, and how many clients paid me. But I couldn't control any of that. I couldn't force people to call me, schedule a session, show up, or hand me their money.

I didn't want to force them to either. I wanted them to be eager and willing to work with me and hand me money because I help them live better lives. I knew it was pointless worrying about things outside of my control, and I needed to devote all my time, energy, and attention to the things I could control, like being an exceptional therapist, giving clients an outstanding experience working with me, and asking for client feedback so I could keep improving. So, I ditched the profit plan. I stopped thinking about how much money I wanted to make because I couldn't control that. I used my mind in a different and better way by starting to think about how I could make every client's experience with me a 10/10.

I shifted away from my profit goals and focused on my service goals because I could control how I showed up for potential and current clients. Rather than focusing on getting more clients, I focused on loving up on the ones I already had by reaching out to them in between sessions to let them know I was thinking of them, sending "thank you" cards to new clients for having the courage to seek help from me, and creating a swoon-worthy experience for clients from the time they walked into the wellness center to the moment they walked out.

It was like switching out the staple gun for the hammer. It felt counterintuitive to forget about the profit plan when my goal was to make more money, but by doing so, I was able to do better work. My clients felt the love and started gushing about how incredible their experience was with me. Before I knew it, I was getting tons of new referrals every week from people who had heard I was the best therapist in the area to work with. My schedule filled up without me having to resort to sleazy sales tactics. I got more clients wanting to work with me than I had time slots for, and I blew my profit plan goals out of the water.

Using my mind to fixate on monetary gain didn't work for me. It made the job so hard and painful. Using my mind to focus on helping, serving, and wowing clients worked wonders and made the job feel as pleasurable as sipping on a glass of Chardonnay while lounging in my favorite twenty-year-old sweatshirt, flipping through the pages of a new library book.

It may seem counterintuitive to *not* focus on making more money, but that's the way it works. The most valuable tool you have in your toolbox is your mind. You decide how to use your time, what to focus on, how to perceive your situation, how to approach problems, how to engage and interact with people, how to respond to situations, how to spend your money, and what you do for money. If you're not where you'd like to be financially, it's time to switch out the tools, baby!

Here are some unhelpful ways you might be using your mind as a tool when it comes to your money:

- Focusing and ruminating on how much (or little) money you earn.
- Setting unrealistic/lofty financial goals for yourself.
- Kicking yourself in the ass when you don't meet those goals.
- Devoting time, energy, and attention to things you can't control.
- Valuing yourself based on the amount of money you earn, how much you have saved, or the amount of debt you do/don't have.
- Putting pressure on yourself to work longer and/or harder when you don't make as much money as you planned.
- Thinking it's okay to spend money as soon as you get it.
- Spending most of your time fantasizing about what you'll do with all the money you wish you had.
- Letting your mind run wild with a bazillion ideas of "easy ways" to make more money.
- Focusing on everything going wrong in your financial life instead of what's working well.

It's time to put all those tools away and pull out better ones.

Here are some helpful ways you can use your mind as a tool when it comes to your money:

- Focus your time, energy, and attention on honing your skills, mastering your craft, and becoming the best at what you do.
- Set realistic intentions about what tasks you want to accomplish in any given period of time.
- Give yourself credit for trying, even when you aren't making the money you want, and keep experimenting with different ways of delivering great value to others.
- Devote your time, energy, and attention only to things you can control. (You can only control *your* thoughts, feelings, behaviors, and responses. Nobody else's.)
- Value yourself based on your skills, knowledge, experience, and the way you treat others.
- Make time for work and for play so you can stay sane, happy, and avoid burnout.
- Keep as much money as possible once you receive it. (Don't splurge on stuff that isn't important to you!)
- Spend most of your time making plans for how you'll show up in the world as your best self.
- Reel in your mind and focus on just *one* really great way to make more money (and actually do it).
- Maintain an attitude of gratitude for all that you already have and the good fortune that currently exists in your life.

Chapter 16

Your Mind is Like a Puppy

When my German Shepherd, Clover, was a puppy, my husband and I spent a tremendous amount of time training her. We were preparing her to be a certified therapy dog who would work with me in my clinical practice.

She was a typical puppy who got into lots of mischief. If we left her outside unattended, she'd wander off. She'd sniff anything that seemed interesting in that moment and veer off the beaten path to distant places in pursuit of the next rabbit poop pile she could roll in.

If we didn't keep a close eye on her, she'd dig up all the landscape tarp, spread the mulch all over the yard, and dig up the newly-planted dogwood tree. That happened FOUR times. Lord only knows how that tree managed to survive Clover's brutal attacks.

While I really hated her habit of getting all stunk up and destroying the landscaping, I expected this behavior because that's what puppies do. Puppies wander around, and without direction or guidance, they get into a lot of trouble.

When I was in the midst of my financial hot mess, I started giving a lot of thought to the way I was thinking about money and discovered that the mind is also like a puppy. I let my thoughts about money wander all over the place, without direction or guidance, and didn't bother to see if they were rational or not. My thoughts about my financial life went unattended, and before I knew it, I got myself into a heap of trouble by thinking I didn't deserve to raise my rates, that I'd never pay off all my debt (so why try), and I should give away a lot of free advice so people would eventually want to buy from me.

Those thoughts led to feelings of low self-worth and hopelessness that I'd ever live debt free. I felt resentful about working my ass off but not making any money. Those feelings led to settling for less than I deserved, procrastinating paying down my debt, and inconsistently delivering valuable content to prospective clients.

My mind was overflowing with junk, low-quality, completely irrational thoughts. When I figured that out, I began contemplating how to challenge those automatic thoughts and gain more control over them. I thought back to Clover.

The upside to Clover's personality was that she liked learning new tricks. She was eager for a challenge and enjoyed the rewards given to her for following our instructions, but she didn't learn overnight. The first time I told her to "sit," she chased a squirrel. The next attempt to teach this basic command involved me plopping her butt down in the grass, giving the verbal command, and immediately rewarding her with a treat. Success! Or so I thought. That was short-lived. She hopped up after her snack and started chasing her tail. I couldn't get her to stop for a solid ten minutes. I knew Clover was smart, and I was determined to teach her how to be an obedient member of our family. I saw great potential in her, and I was confident that given the right training, she'd make an excellent therapy dog.

So, we kept working on it over and over again. Every day, we'd practice sitting, lying down, heeling, speaking, and shaking. Finally, after all that practice and all of my patience maxed out, she got it. Now Clover is reliable and consistent. She knows what to do and when to do it. She's obedient and follows all my commands. Well, about ninety-eight percent of them. Everyone has bad days. She served clients at my wellness center for many years and added tremendous value to people's lives.

I trained Clover to work for me, not against me. Yet, she wouldn't be able to do any of this had I not taught her how. Had I not given her the time, effort, patience, direction, and guidance, she'd still be that whimsical puppy who wanders off and rolls in shit, which would've driven me bananas.

Just like Clover needed time and repetition to become obedient, your mind requires just the same. If you don't train your mind, it will wander around aimlessly, fixating on what's going wrong instead of what's going right and causing you a boatload of mental money drama, which stinks as bad as Clover did when she rolled in bunny poo.

However, if you practice retraining your brain to think about your money in new and better ways, and repeat the process over and over again (rewarding yourself when you do a good job), your mind will form a new habit. In turn, you'll start to see your money in healthy, rational ways. The secret is to recognize automatic, irrational thoughts as you experience them. First, you have to become aware of the cognitive distortion, and then you have to challenge it.

I bet you've experienced cognitive distortions more than once in your life, which is totally normal. When you have thoughts like *I'll never make the kind of money I want* or *I'm a complete failure when it comes to controlling my spending*, you feel bad about yourself, your money, and your life. But you want to feel nothing but love for your money and love for yourself because you and your money are amazing!

To solve this problem, you need to recognize a cognitive distortion as being an irrational thought, challenge that thought, and reframe it. Holding a more rational thought in your mind will help you feel better about money and focus on what matters.

Like this:

Cognitive distortion: "I should be making $10,000 a month by now."
Emotional consequence: Feeling like a failure in your career and guilty for not being farther along.
Challenge/Reframe: "It would be nice if I was making $10,000 a month by now, but it requires advocating for a pay raise and showing why I deserve it. I'm going to keep a log of all the ways I contribute to the company and request a pay raise."
Emotional consequence: Feeling hopeful that you'll make more money in time and committed to putting in the work.

See how reframing the thought and putting a different spin on it makes you feel completely different about your situation? When you feel positive about your abilities and your potential to make more money, you have more focus, drive, determination, and ambition, which results in more action, better decisions, and more productivity. The result is more money, confidence, connections, and success.

Do you see how powerful your thoughts are? Everything begins as a thought. Everything! Every successful business, every dollar earned, every product or service ever offered, every book ever written, and every dream you've seen come true all started out as a thought or an idea.

Therefore, your thoughts need to be of the highest quality. They need to be completely rational and grounded in positivity and optimism. Simply put, you need to control your thoughts or your thoughts will control you.

Chapter 17

Money Mindset

Now, let's pop open the hood of your mind and take a look at your thoughts about money because they will reveal a lot about the quality of your money relationship. Some people say we all have "a type": a particular kind of person we're attracted to. Many say that if you have "a type," you form patterns of gravitating toward the people who match that type.

Maybe you're like me and gravitate toward the tall, dark, and handsome type. Maybe you're more of a blond hair and blue eyes kind of girl. Or maybe you go for the rebels, or the "too cool for school" type, or the emotionally unavailable kind. The funny, down-to-earth, cuddly like a teddy bear type might be what turns you on. If you look back over your romantic relationships, you could discover that you've dated many different people, but they were all sorta the same because they all fit your "type."

If the type of people you're attracted to fit well with your personality, your relationships were probably pretty happy and healthy. But if you dated rebels all the time, you might have found yourself with more than one broken heart. Now, let me ask you this: When it comes to your money mindset, do you have a type?

Most of us fall into one of two camps. You're either the *scarcity* mindset type or you're the *abundance* mindset type. Let's look at both. An abundance mindset is based on the belief that there are plenty of resources (love, money, opportunities, customers/clients, food, etc.) for everyone and that we can all have these resources without taking them away from someone else. An abundance mindset is one in which there is trust that all of your needs will be met and that the gifts that life has to offer are of unlimited supply.

A scarcity mindset is just the opposite. It's the belief that there is a limited amount of love, money, opportunity, etc., and you have to get it before it's gone or fight for your fair share. There's also an underlying belief that if you grab hold of more money or opportunities, you're taking them away from someone else, which makes you feel guilty.

Believing that there's enough money to go around allows you to enjoy your money without feeling guilty about depriving someone else of it. Knowing that there's an unlimited amount of money, resources, and opportunities eliminates a feeling of competition and frees up your precious energy. It allows you to direct your energy toward productive action instead of wasting it on trying to protect yourself from losing what you already have. Having an abundance mindset makes you feel calm, safe, secure, and blessed. Having a scarcity mindset makes you feel scared, suspicious, defensive, and unlucky. Just like how a cuddly type makes you feel safe and warm in the relationship and how a mysterious badass type makes you feel insecure and on edge in the relationship.

You may not be able to change the type of partner you're attracted to, but you absolutely can change the type of money mindset you maintain. There's no way you can genuinely love and accept your financial situation if you're always thinking that you'll never have enough or you're constantly worried that your money will be here one day and gone the next. If you want your money relationship to thrive, you've got to weed out all thoughts of scarcity and limitation and shift to a mindset of abundance. Let me show you how.

Chapter 18

Your Mind is Like a Garden

Think of your mind like a garden. Your thoughts are seeds planted in the soil of your mind, and with time, those thoughts will grow into realities. You'll harvest a variety of experiences in your life based on the thoughts that were planted. We know that if you plant a carrot seed in the soil, carrots will grow. We have full faith and trust it will be so. Therefore, we don't question the process.

The same process applies to money. If you plant thoughts of abundance, financial success, and income-producing opportunities in your mind, you'll experience abundance, financial success, and increased income in your life. If you plant thoughts of scarcity, financial struggle, and expenses always exceeding income in your mind, you'll experience all of that in your life. We know and trust that will be the case. You experience what you expect to experience. You reap what you sow.

You might be thinking, *Hot damn! The mind is so freakin' powerful!* Or you could be thinking, *Hold up. Are you saying that I can make more money simply by changing my thoughts? That seems ridonkulous.* That's exactly what I'm saying, and it's not ridonkulous. In fact, scientific evidence and real-life experience prove it. Your mind has the power to grow a garden of money, as much as you want, to "feed" you for life. But all gardens require tending. A garden doesn't plant itself. It needs adequate soil, water, and sunlight. The weeds need to be pulled regularly so they don't take over the whole damn thing and squeeze the life out of your precious crops.

To be more literal, if you want to experience financial abundance in your life, you need to do meaningful work you believe in to earn money. You need to believe that you can and will make as much money as you want through that work. You need to think that you deserve to receive that money. You need to remove any thoughts from your mind that say otherwise so limiting beliefs don't sabotage your financial success. And when the money comes to you, you need to take good care of it by giving it a job (in your spending plan).

Are you jumping with joy at this revelation and doing backflips of excitement because you now know that you have the power to create all the money you want? Or are you stomping your feet, scrunching your face, and screaming, "Why the hell didn't anyone tell me this sooner?! I could be a millionaire by now if I'd known this!"

Wanna know why nobody told you this sooner? Most people aren't in control of their thoughts, so they allow their minds to operate in "default mode," planting thought seeds at random and hoping for the best. It's like taking a bucket full of seeds and spreading them around the yard. Then, they just sit back and wait to see if anything grows without doing anything to help the process and never knowing what might pop up. Because most people aren't in control of their thoughts, they don't grow a harvest of money in their lives.

But this doesn't have to be you. You have the power to create the financial life you want, and you do this by only holding in your mind what you want to experience in reality. If you don't want to live paycheck-to-paycheck, don't keep telling yourself that you don't deserve a raise! If those thoughts come into your mind, weed them out! Replace negative thoughts of lack with thoughts of abundance because that's what you want to experience.

WARNING: Your mind has a natural tendency to gravitate toward the negative.

Ever notice how it's so easy to pick out what's going wrong in your financial situation? It's easy to see what you wish was different or better, but it's hard to see what's going well, what's working, and how much you've grown. That's part of being human, but it's important for you to train your mind to focus on the good because when the mind gets all wrapped up in the negative, it creates a lot of weeds in your garden.

The weeds hinder the growth of the good thoughts you want to nurture and harvest. They take over the soil and steal important nutrients from the good you're trying to grow in your life. If you don't eliminate the negative thoughts about your money and your ability to earn and manage money, the weeds will take over and kill the financial harvest you're trying to produce.

Part of the human experience involves continually working on weeding out the garden of your mind. This is work you must tend to regularly in order to live the life of your dreams. To do this, you have to practice shifting negative thoughts to positive ones. You have to consciously and deliberately seek out what's going well and identify the abundance in your life that you can be grateful for. The weeding process involves eliminating the negative, limiting thoughts that keep you from experiencing your heart's desires. It takes work, practice, and self-discipline, but it allows your wildest dreams to grow and manifest in your life.

One distinction to make here is that, sometimes, really bad things happen to us in life. We become sick or injured. We lose someone we love. We experience debilitating depression or anxiety. By no means am I suggesting that you "just think positive" or look on the bright side when you experience hardship, pain, or loss in your life. To do so would be practicing "toxic positivity" and denying yourself the opportunity to authentically feel valid emotions. You have full permission to give yourself time to feel all the feels before working on shifting your thoughts in a more positive direction.

Chapter 19

Planting Your Money Garden

Planting your money garden is easy. Here are the steps:

1. Pick out your seeds.
Reflect on what you really, really want. Get clear on your desires and be as specific as possible. If you aren't sure, revisit chapter five and answer the questions I posed. Write down what you want to experience in life, how much money you want to make, and what you want to do with it. These are the "seeds" you want to plant in your mind.

2. Plant your seeds.
Look at your desires—the things you want to have and experience. Hold those in your mind as if you have them NOW. This is going to feel weird, and your mind might start arguing with you by saying, "You're lying to yourself! You don't have x, y, and z now!" Tune out your inner critic, and stay focused on what you want. Try to find examples as

evidence that you have **some** of what you want now or a sign that it's coming to you.

3. Spread fertilizer on your money garden.
Things grow better when they have food. When it comes to feeding the money seeds you've planted, desire and trust are the best fertilizers. You want to stir up a burning desire to attract the things you want into your life. You can do this by imagining how you'll feel once you get those things. Having full faith and trust that you will receive or experience those things also fertilizes your money seeds. You don't need to know exactly how they will come to be. Just believe that everything you want is growing in your life, even if you can't see it yet. Think about it. Carrots grow underground, out of sight, and you don't think anything's happening until their little green tops pop up. Money is like that, too. Just because you can't see progress, it doesn't mean it's not happening.

4. Pull out the weeds.
Thoughts of doubt, skepticism, impatience, and unworthiness are bound to pop up in your mind. Other people will act like weeds, too. There are lots of naysayers out there who will try to convince you that this is all hocus pocus nonsense, filling you with self-doubt. These negative thoughts are weeds, and they need to be eliminated immediately to keep your money crop healthy and growing. Be on the lookout for these weeds (negative thoughts of lack/limitation) and replace them with positive/abundant thoughts. Keep believing and trusting that it's only a matter of time until you receive what you desire.

5. Harvest your money crop.

When you receive what you desire (because you absolutely will), you'll want to recognize yourself for the hard work you put into tending to your money garden and extend gratitude and appreciation for your bountiful harvest. Enjoy the money (or whatever it is that you wanted) without feeling guilty or ashamed. Don't entertain any ideas about not deserving it or that you're taking something from someone else. You planted the money seeds. You fertilized them with your desire. You did the hard work of pulling out the weeds (negative thoughts). You earned this harvest!

Now, you might be thinking, *Okay, Nicole, first you told me my mind is like a tool. Then you told me my mind is like a puppy. After that, you said my mind is like a garden. Which one is it?* Great question! I'm so glad you asked!

Your mind is like all of the above. I like to offer up several different analogies to help you understand your mind better because, let's face it, the mind is a complicated thing that most people just don't get. And I believe in different strokes for different folks. Maybe one analogy resonates with you better than another. Go with the one that makes the most sense to you.

I also do this to make an important point: *perception is everything*. There's one main point that I'm driving home here: Your mind is powerful and can be used to create the life you want. I looked at this point from three different angles, described it in three different ways, and provided three different examples to illustrate the idea, and each one is true. Different, but true.

You perceive money matters in one way; your partner perceives money matters in another, and your BFF perceives money matters in a completely different way. You're all right. You're all speaking your truth about money based on your individual perception of it. But as you've already learned, your perception of money colors the way you think, feel, and behave with money and determines what your money relationship and financial future will look like.

If you're perceiving your money relationship in a way that makes you feel guilt, shame, embarrassment, hopelessness, and fear, it's time to use your mind as a tool and shift your perception of money to something that serves you better.

Hopefully by now, you're coming to accept your mental power. When you discover how powerful your mind truly is and develop the ability to use your mind intentionally, your relationship with money and your financial life will transform.

Money Therapy Assignment

Tracking Cognitive Distortions: identifying automatic, irrational thoughts and challenge them so you can keep your "money-making mental garden" weed-free.

This assignment is all about getting some practice with identifying cognitive distortions and challenging irrational thoughts so you can kick feeling crappy to the curb and focus on your money love affair. As you move through the week, pay attention to how you're feeling. Notice any negative feelings popping up for you and write them down. (Examples include anxiety, fear, guilt, shame, embarrassment, anger, and frustration.)

Then, briefly describe the actual event that led to the unpleasant emotion. Next, look at the list of cognitive distortions in chapter 14 and pick out which one you're experiencing in that moment (i.e. all-or-nothing thinking or mental filter). It's possible to experience multiple cognitive distortions at the same time too! Jot down the distortions that are coming up for you.

Finally, challenge the cognitive distortion by writing down more rational thoughts about the situation. (Examples include replacing "should" with "it would be nice," "I wish" to reframe "should statements," or pointing out positive aspects of the situation instead of just focusing on the negative.)

This is not an easy assignment! Just like Clover didn't learn to sit on the first day, you won't learn how to challenge irrational thoughts overnight either. Practice makes *progress*, so just keep practicing.

PART V: BELIEFS: SELF-WORTH DETERMINES NET WORTH

Chapter 20

Toxic Money Beliefs

What are **beliefs**? Beliefs are made-up stories and attitudes based on assumptions you've made about how the world works. Let me highlight something important: They are **made-up stories**. Fantasies. Illusions. Not real. But beliefs feel very real, so we take them as truth. We rarely question our beliefs and how they affect our feelings and behaviors. Since we don't often examine our beliefs or question the assumptions we make about ourselves, others, our money, and the world, our beliefs can run amuck and create big problems in our lives without us even being aware of what's going on.

How do beliefs form? Beliefs are formed by your interpretation of your experiences, the messages you've received from others (peers, parents, mentors, community leaders, the media), your personal values, and your expectations. They form without you having any conscious awareness of it, and once a belief is formed, it's there forever, or until you recognize you don't like it and do the work to change the belief.

Another important thing to know about beliefs is that they serve as filters and influence the way you process information. All day, every day, you've got all sorts of information flying at you; so much that your mind can't take it all in. Your mind has to sort out what's important and what isn't in a split second and choose what to pay attention to and what to ignore so it doesn't get overloaded.

Beliefs act as filters that influence what you pay attention to, what you ignore, what's let in, and what's kept out. That's how a belief can stay intact forever. Once a belief is established, you constantly search for evidence that will support the belief and ignore any evidence that contradicts it because if you paid attention to evidence that proved the belief to be false, you'd have to change the belief. Beliefs don't want to be erased from your mind. They want to stick around, be in charge, and call the shots on how you perceive things. Those little rascals.

Now, if the belief is healthy and serves you well, then you want those beliefs to hang around forever! But if the belief is toxic and creating a bunch of problems for you, then you have to dig in there and change the belief.

Consider this example:
Based on the messages I heard in graduate school and from colleagues, I formed the assumption that therapists can't make much money. My belief would look like this: "I'm in the wrong field to make good money."

Then, I'd constantly search for evidence to support this belief. The evidence I'd pay attention to would look like this: "Therapists often work in community mental health clinics, which are low-paying jobs. The field is dedicated to public service. People don't really value mental health services. I'm destined to earn peanuts because my work isn't valued."

If this is my belief, and I keep paying attention to evidence that supports it, I won't believe I have the ability to make good money and that will become a self-fulfilling prophecy. I will actively (and unconsciously) create that outcome for myself. But if I recognize the belief is toxic and keeping me from earning the money I want, I can rescript the story and start finding evidence to support the new, healthier version of the belief.

Like this:

New belief: "Many therapists and mental health providers make GREAT money, and I can too."

Evidence to support it: "CEOs of nonprofits make a lot of money. Therapists in private practice determine their own earning potential. There are numerous authors and researchers in the mental health field who make a boatload of money. Freakin' Brene Brown is a social worker/therapist and look at all the success she's had! I can have that kind of success too!"

As you can see, your beliefs are a really big deal, especially when it comes to your money. If you're carrying around toxic money beliefs, they'll influence the way you think, feel, and behave with money. Those toxic money beliefs aren't true or factual. They're just made up. Worse than that though, toxic beliefs cause a whole boatload of FEAR.

FEAR you will fail.

FEAR you won't make enough money to support yourself and your family.

FEAR you'll be forced to work for a terrible boss or stay in a job you hate.

FEAR you'll have to compromise your values or integrity to earn the money you want.

FEAR you'll have to lose something valuable to you in exchange for money.

FEAR that you'll have to fight for your fair share and get as much money as you can, or you'll miss out completely.

The fear is what keeps you awake at night. It's also what stands between you and a loving relationship with your money. You either fear your money or you love your money. You can't have it both ways. Fear is your biggest barrier to financial freedom. Not your spouse. Not your kids. Not your age. Not your credentials. Not your job. Not your gender.

What you need to know about fear is this:

Fear is normal.

Fear is a life-long companion that will always be there.

Fear ensures your survival by giving you the ability to perceive danger.

Sometimes your perception of danger is false, and fear flares up when you don't need it to.

Fear isn't necessarily bad. You just have to know how to deal with it.

1. Don't let fear drive you.

Fear is welcome to come along for the ride, but it belongs in the backseat, not guiding the direction of your life. Push fear to the side so it doesn't stand between you and your money.

2. Feel the fear, and do it anyway.

It takes courage to ask for a raise, talk with your partner about money, cut back expenses, and pay off debt. It's gonna get really uncomfortable. Feel the feels. Do hard things.

3. *Let go of what's holding you back.*
Fear might be telling you things like, "Oh no, you can't do that. That's too risky and too scary. That will spark a financial catastrophe, crush your soul, and ruin your reputation. Play it safe!"

Have a little heart-to-heart with fear. Let your fear know that you appreciate it looking out for you, but you got this. You're not going to do anything that will get yourself killed. Everything will be okay. Then kindly ask your fear to pipe down and chillax so you can let go of what's holding you back and move on to bigger and better things. Don't look back.

Before I did Money Therapy^R with myself, my money relationship looked like a dumpster fire. Part of the reason for that was because of the unhealthy underlying beliefs I had about myself, money, and the potential (or lack thereof) to achieve financial independence. I came from a "broken family." I had a single mom and never met my father. My grandparents raised me and brought me up with their values and money beliefs. Their idea of living a wealthy life didn't include big houses or fancy cars. It was about growing fresh vegetables in the garden, putting in a swimming pool after years of saving, and paying for me to take piano lessons every week.

Because my family life wasn't "normal" and my dad wasn't a doctor like the fathers of the girls I went to school with, I fell into the "misfit clique." I was quiet, private, and creative. None of my peers knew much about me, so they made stuff up. Some said I was poor and lived in a trailer park. Others said I had money because I wore brand name clothes to school. Even though there were other unpopular, poor misfits in the clique I was assigned to by my peers, I didn't feel like I fit in anywhere with them, either. I spent most of my life feeling embarrassed, ashamed, and unworthy of being happy, wealthy, or loved.

Despite my insecurities and introversion, I had a burning desire for a better life. I wanted to be happy and make an impact in the world. I wanted to do something special with my life. I wanted to have money to travel and experience new things. I didn't want to struggle like my mom or grandparents. I didn't want to be kept from living my dreams because I couldn't afford them.

Yet, deep down, I didn't believe I was worthy of being rich. How could I be worthy? I came from nothing. It seemed like my own parents didn't really want me. I didn't have close friends. People gossiped about me, and I could only imagine what the kids at school thought of me. Nope, there was no way I was worthy of making a lot of money, having nice things, or obtaining the freedom and independence to live my dream life. But I wanted it. I wanted it so damn bad.

I figured that there must be a way to earn worth. Maybe if I were good, worked hard, paid my dues, and did all the right things, then I might be worthy of making the kind of money I wanted. I spent over ten years trying to shed my misfit identity and become worthy of living my dreams. I did everything I was "supposed" to do. Got my education. Got a big-shot job with a nice salary. Got a man. Got engaged.

And yet, every step of the way, I felt restless, stressed out, and angry. It wasn't what I had pictured for myself.

It wasn't until the relationship I was in at the time ended abruptly and my job burnt me out that I was all alone with nothing to do but soul search. Despite all my hard work, why wasn't I making the kind of money I wanted? Why was I still struggling to pay bills? Where did I go wrong?

In the moments of quiet, in between the tears, I discovered that I was worthy all along. It never mattered where I came from, how people treated me in the past, or what anyone thought of me. What mattered was that I believed I was worthy of money, living debt-free, freedom, and independence. It was my own beliefs about myself and labeling myself as an undeserving misfit that kept me from having what I wanted. At the time though, I didn't believe any of that. I felt like I was broke as a joke and couldn't afford anything. These feelings made me start overcompensating and the way I went about it wasn't pretty.

Perception is everything. Your interpretation of your experiences and the meaning you attach to them determines the quality of your life experience and the quality of your relationship with money. Your past experiences with money might not all be stellar, which might be why you don't feel all warm and fuzzy for your money.

So, you've made mistakes with your money in the past. Who hasn't? Maybe you weren't so nice to your money, falling for the persuasion and charm of advertisements and spending recklessly. Because you've had some pretty bad money relationships in the past, you might believe that you don't deserve to have a good money relationship now.

Do you feel like you don't really deserve to be rich? I've so been there, and that feeling of not being worthy felt like a fact and sabotaged my relationship with money. Feelings are funny. They often aren't true or even rational. Negative feelings that are accepted as facts undermine your success in creating the life you want for yourself.

MONEY TRUTH: You don't get what you deserve. You get what you *believe* you deserve.

There's a big difference. If you believe you deserve a pumpkin spice latte today, chances are you'll treat yourself to one. If you believe you deserve a week off to hike the Appalachian Trail, chances are you'll take the trip. If you don't believe you deserve either of those things, there's no way you're gonna get 'em because you won't take the necessary steps to bring them to yourself. Why? Because you just "aren't worthy." The belief that you don't deserve the things you really want keeps you making excuses for why you can't have your dream life instead of taking action to create the life you want.

Beliefs are powerful. They can either make or break your money relationship. Beware because beliefs hide deep beneath the surface of your psyche. You can't easily spot them, but they're always there, either working for you or against you. Let's take a closer look at what beliefs are, how they come into existence in the first place, what they do, and how they can affect your money relationship.

Chapter 21

Feelings Aren't Facts

When I was in college, I worked three jobs and was still broke as shit. I took a full class load studying psychology, worked as a bank teller fifteen hours a week, worked at the local women's shelter as a legal advocate where I filed protection from abuse orders for victims of domestic violence and sexual assault, and worked at Bath & Body Works at night and on weekends where I gave free "hand facials" and came home smelling like cucumber melon every night.

I worked a lot, but minimum wage was crap money, and I barely had enough every month to make my car payment, put gas in the thing to get me back and forth to school and work, and go out to eat with my boyfriend (because I was *not* eating dining hall food). I never had any money for anything.

My roommate, Kathleen, would always take random trips to Walmart at one a.m. for fun, and I'd always tag along because I had nothing better to do. She'd load her cart with

Cheetos, M&M'S, the newest editions of *Cosmo* and *Vogue*, nail polish, new shampoo, perfume, cute fuzzy slippers, and romantic comedies on Blu-ray for us to watch in our dorm room. She always seemed to have the money for whatever she wanted, whenever she wanted to buy it, while I, empty-handed, just tagged along beside her cart.

I loved those late-night shopping trips with Kathleen because they were so ridiculous. Fun fact, she always felt bad for me and bought me a little something. Being so broke made me feel sorry for myself and wonder why the hell I didn't have any goddamn money, especially because I was working my ass off. The kicker: Kathleen didn't have a job. Her parents deposited money into her account every week.

It felt like I was the only one who was broke, and I wallowed in self-pity. My mind filled with garbage thoughts about how "I'd never get ahead," "I'd always be poor," and "I'd never have what I wanted." I'd never pay off my car, have my own Coach purse (the status symbol I drooled over at that time in my life), and never get my own apartment where I would finally be able to undress without trying to hide my naked body from my roommate. I also told myself that I'd never get a good-paying job and was probably doomed to work at Bath & Body Works for the rest of my life. The best I could hope for was to be promoted to manager and earn $11/hour instead of $8. My money mindset was pathetic.

I'd get invitations to go do cool stuff with my friends, and I'd turn them down because I "couldn't afford it." I admired the dazzling rhinestone earrings worn by the girl who sat next to me in class, but I wouldn't buy a pair for myself because I "couldn't afford it." All day, every day, no matter what, I couldn't afford it. My mind was full of trash money talk. Then, something incredible happened.

The president of the psychological association announced that the department was taking a trip to Europe that summer and I could tour Europe with my class for two weeks. All I had to do was get a passport and come up with $3,000. I was in! There was no freakin' way I was going to miss out on seeing the Eiffel Tower's shimmering lights at night or give up devouring fresh crepes covered with melted chocolate and banana slices. I also wouldn't pass up the opportunity to see Venice, Austria, Munich, Berlin, Amsterdam, and Rome. I needed $3,000? No problem. Consider it done.

I scrimped and saved, happily worked extra hours, and crocheted handmade scarves to sell to the old ladies at church to raise money for the trip. I was determined to come up with the money for Europe, and I did it. Suddenly, I wasn't broke anymore. I had money, and I wasn't feeling sorry for myself either. I couldn't afford to pay off my car, buy a Coach purse, AND pay for the Europe trip, but I had enough for the trip, and that's what I valued most of all. I could afford it.

The odd thing was that I wasn't making a whole lot more than I was before I knew about the Europe trip. The thing that had changed was I now had a purpose for my money: a goal that was important to me. I started taking better care of my money so I could experience my dream of traveling to Europe.

Here's the thing: When you really, really, really want something, you'll find the money for it. You'll make it happen. You'll do whatever it takes to get it. If you're "meh" about something, feel like you can live without it, and it's not that important to you, you'll tell yourself you can't afford it. Feeling like you've got no money, you can't afford jack shit, and you'll never have the things you want is going to make you behave in alignment with those thoughts. You will actively manifest the reality you don't want for yourself.

What stories are you telling about yourself? What labels do you use to describe yourself in your own mind? What fears do those false stories stir up in you? Maybe you're worried that you'll have to give something up in exchange for your money, like not having time with loved ones, leisure or travel time, or time for self-care. Maybe you fear you'll lose something, or someone, precious to you if you have more money, like fearing your partner will leave you if you get "too successful," "too famous," or "too rich." Perhaps you fear that you'll lose friends because they'll see you as a "rich bitch" whom they can no longer relate to.

The stories you tell yourself and the beliefs you hold create a whole slew of feelings that aren't always pleasant. Those feelings feel like facts. They feel like proven truths that are bound to happen in reality. But feelings aren't facts. Beliefs aren't facts. They may feel that way, but they're just made-up stories.

Unhealthy, limiting beliefs can torment you and poison your money relationship. Toxic money beliefs can make you fear and resent your money instead of loving and appreciating it. So, if you really want to make this new love affair with money super juicy, you have to gain awareness of your toxic money beliefs and see them for what they are: Illusions that aren't serving you or your money relationship well.

Here's an equation to keep in mind:

AWARENESS + ACTION = CHANGE

You're tired of struggling financially. You're ready to ditch the beliefs keeping you broke and change your relationship with money for the better. But before you can create an action plan to bring about that change, you have to gain awareness about what isn't working and figure out exactly what needs to be changed. In this case, you need to figure out which stories need to be rescripted so you can create a healthier version of the story; one that serves you and your money well and leads to a passionate, long-lasting love affair. The assignment that you'll complete at the end of this section will help you discover the unhealthy beliefs you have about money and give you clarity on what needs to change.

Chapter 22

Rescripting Beliefs

Here are some examples of common toxic money beliefs you might have (which dredge up icky feelings) and healthier versions of each (which spark positive, "yay!" vibes):

ICKY BELIEF: "If I make more money, I'm depriving someone else of it."
YAY! BELIEF: "Money is being made every day, and there's plenty to go around."

ICKY BELIEF: "I have to give up/be away from/lose relationships with my family & friends in order to make money."
YAY! BELIEF: "I can have both. Having money will allow me to be more selective about when and how much I work."

ICKY BELIEF: "I don't deserve money because I came from a poor family."

YAY! BELIEF: "I'm not my family. I chose my own path. I am great at what I do and have a lot to offer."

ICKY BELIEF: "If I have money, I will squander it."
YAY! BELIEF: "I'm learning how to manage money well and will continue to get better at using my money wisely."

ICKY BELIEF: "If I make a lot of money, I'm taking it away from other people who work just as hard as I do."
YAY! BELIEF: "Everyone is responsible for earning what they believe they deserve. Other people determine their earnings, not me. The only thing I can control is what I expect for myself."

ICKY BELIEF: "Money is fragile, and it will eventually stop flowing into my business."
YAY! BELIEF: "There will always be money. I've always had enough, and I will plan and prepare for the inevitable ebbs and flows."

Here's the deal on beliefs: Beliefs need supportive evidence in order for them to stay intact. Imagine a table. The tabletop is the belief. The legs of the table are the pieces of evidence that hold up the tabletop. The legs serve as the evidence that supports the belief, making it seem true. You can see that the evidence you find to support the belief might be a silly excuse to stay in your comfort zone instead of changing your life in a major way.

Too old to go back to school? That's an excuse. People in their sixties go back to school. People are set in their ways by age forty? That's an excuse. Where did that bogus rule even come from? You need a new table, love.

To rescript your toxic beliefs, you need to create a new, healthier belief and make it your tabletop. Try this, "I am capable of changing my life in a major way." Eh, hold up. Did you feel that? When you read the new belief, did you feel a little tug, like your mind immediately doubted it? Does that new belief feel like a *lie*?

Well, guess what? It is a lie, but so is the toxic belief that you're too old to change your life in major ways. BOTH ARE LIES! BELIEFS ARE LIES. The difference is that one lie makes you feel hopeless and stuck while the other lie makes you feel powerful and motivated.

You're going to have beliefs no matter what, which means you're essentially always lying to yourself. You might as well lie to yourself in a way that makes you feel good and gets you the results you want instead of lying to yourself in ways that damage your money relationship, self-esteem, and financial success.

In order to get a new, healthier belief to stick, you have to find evidence to support the new belief—new legs to keep your table upright, so to speak. Like this: "I saw in an article that a woman in her sixties just got a bachelor's degree," or "I made a major change in my life three years ago, and I'm not much older now than I was then." You get the point. It's the *evidence* that makes the belief feel true instead of it feeling like a lie. Now, you'll need to search and find some compelling evidence to hardwire your new money-loving beliefs.

One more thing before you leap into action: The brain loves habit, repetition, and routine. It likes doing the same thing over and over again and knowing what to expect. Whenever you try to form a new habit or think in a new way, you're going to experience *resistance*.

Your brain will be like, "Woah there! We don't do things like *that*! We do things like *this*! Go back to the old way, the familiar way!" Then you gotta be like, "Hold up, brain. I'm the boss, and we do things like this now. Get with the program. Try it! You'll like it!"

You might have to have that conversation with yourself about a gazillion times before your brain catches on, settles into the new routine, and starts thinking differently about money. With time, a new way of thinking will become a new habit. Let's get to work on that.

Money Therapy Assignment

Restructuring Limiting Beliefs: hardwiring new, money-loving beliefs.

Now you'll work on re-scripting your limiting beliefs. The goal is to transform limiting beliefs into healthier versions that will serve your money relationship well, so you can experience big changes in your financial life.

Rescripting beliefs is a process that has three steps:

1. Look back at the examples of toxic money beliefs (icky beliefs) presented in this chapter and jot down the ones you're experiencing.
2. Create a new, healthier money belief (yay! beliefs).
3. Find evidence to support the new yay! belief.

The work doesn't stop there. You have to keep thinking about your new, healthy money beliefs and search for evidence to uphold these beliefs while resisting the pull you'll feel to go back to old ways of thinking. Just keep at it, and these new, money-loving beliefs will stick. Below is an example of how you might organize your thoughts to complete the three-step process of rescripting beliefs.

ICKY MONEY BELIEF	YAY! MONEY BELIEF	EVIDENCE TO SUPPORT YAY! BELIEF
Ex: If I make a lot of money, I'll be a "rich bitch."	If I make a lot of money, I'll have the power to do more good in the world.	Oprah has boatloads of money, and she isn't a rich bitch. She gives generously and helps people. I can be like that too.

PART VI: AN OUT-OF-BODY EXPERIENCE WITH MONEY

Chapter 23

A Little Bit of Woo-Woo

Now you know that your thoughts influence your feelings and your feelings influence the way you behave with money. The way you think about money directly affects the quality of your financial life. Most people think of money as material: a piece of paper they can hold in their hands and exchange for goods and services. They think that money is printed in limited supply and there's only so much to go around, which leads to a scarcity mindset. Money is so much more than that. It's not just material; it's also spiritual. This chapter might feel woo-woo to some because what I'm about to share with you is a little "out of this world." Try to stay calm, and don't freak out, because there are some solid wisdom nuggets here that you don't want to miss.

Money is energy, and it's made from the same stuff that made you, the mountains, the sun, and the peanut butter sandwich you had for lunch. Money is simply a gift from whatever power created all people and things, and money is no different than the gift of the sky, water, or air. Just like the sky, water, or air, money is a resource of unlimited supply that's constantly available to you. All the money you could ever imagine is already in existence, and it's waiting for you to use the power of your mind to attract it into your life.

How do you feel when you hear me say that? Maybe you're like, "Cool! I totally feel connected to a higher power, and all this spiritual stuff completely resonates with me!" Or maybe you're like, "Um, I didn't come here to be preached to, and I'm so not religious. Just get back to telling me how to make more money." I feel you, and I'm not here to impose my views on you or make you a "believer." I've learned from experience that having a spiritual relationship can result in massive boosts of love in your money relationship and massive boosts of cash in your bank account. Therefore, exploring all this spiritual stuff is an important part of your money relationship.

Let me make a quick distinction here: Spirituality is *not* religion. Spirituality doesn't make up all sorts of rules for you to follow or demand that you only associate with people who believe the same things as you. Spirituality doesn't insist upon having proof or evidence to sustain a belief in something you can't see. Instead, spirituality empowers you with *choices*. Choose your faith. Choose your beliefs. Choose your desires. Choose the kind of relationship you want with a higher power. So many choices, all of which connect you back to some kind of energy greater than yourself. You can call that energy anything you want. Call it Universe, God, Spirit, Buddha, or Smurf Fairies. Whatever feels good to you, call it that.

I like to call it the Universe, so that's what you'll hear me say from now on when referring to the higher power that created all things. The whole point is that everything that's ever been in existence has come from the Universe, *including* money. So, if you want more money, it's wise to build a rock-solid relationship with the Universe.

Nurturing the spiritual side of your life doesn't have to be complicated or time-consuming. There are some super easy ways to tap into the power of the Universe and use it to attract more money, opportunities, and connections to the right people. Not only does spirituality help you improve your financial life, it also improves resilience in the face of adversity. Research has shown that feeling connected to a higher power helps people overcome trauma and crises better and faster than those who don't. I've seen it firsthand with my therapy clients.

As such, I'm going to teach you some spiritual practices that will help you see that you and your money come from the same place, that you are one with each other, and that you and your money have a lot of similarities. These spiritual practices will help you respect and cherish your money more, without hoarding it or clinging to it. They will help you believe you deserve to have as much money as you want, which is the first step in actually receiving the money you want.

The spiritual practices I'm sharing with you are the same ones I use myself; the ones that helped me get out of a financial rut, multiply my income times five in eight months, pay off all my debt, attract the money for my farmette (like a farm but much smaller and with fewer animals), and fall head-over-heels in love with my money. All I ask is that you stay open-minded as you read this chapter and give these ideas and practices a try. What do you have to lose?

Let me share a personal story from my own experience to illustrate how powerful spiritual practices can be when it comes to attracting money and abundance. It was a sunny spring day, but I was feeling particularly grumbly about my financial situation despite the fair weather. I'd just spent an hour looking at real estate listings, admiring all the big farmhouses on the market and dreaming and drooling at the idea of having acreage, chickens free-ranging in the yard, an in-ground pool for my kids to swim in, and wide-open space for Clover to run. I imagined myself baking decadent desserts in the spacious kitchen and sipping on cocktails with friends as we sat in front of the outdoor fireplace.

I wanted it. I wanted it all **so bad**. I hated where I was living, and it wasn't because the house was small or crappy. It was because I didn't have space. My neighbors were right on top of me. I felt I had zero privacy and living on the side of a mountain didn't make for great playing in the backyard.

The worst part though was that a new house had been built right next door to me and our new neighbor was a living nightmare. He harassed me, screamed at me from his yard daily, and flipped me off any chance he could get. He made bogus complaints to the township about us, causing my family and me an enormous amount of stress. He came onto our property and stole things out of our yard when we weren't home. He was legit unhinged.

We tried to reason with him and involved the police, but nothing changed. I felt anxious, afraid, and on edge every day. I dreaded going home because of that neighbor. I kept my kids inside on beautiful, sunny days because of that neighbor. I knew he wasn't going anywhere, and I wasn't lucky enough for him to move out of the neighborhood. He'd just built that house and moved in a few months prior. If one of us were going to make a move, it would have to be me.

I found myself fantasizing about leaving all that drama behind and moving out to the country, far, far away from all neighbors. Yet, as soon as a hopeful thought entered my mind, it was immediately overtaken by a whole slew of negative thoughts. "There's no way you can afford a house like that, Nicole. You don't have the money. Money doesn't grow on trees. It's impossible."

Then old money baggage reared its ugly head. "What makes you think you deserve a big farmhouse like that? Nobody gets everything they want, especially you. Are you kidding? Your business isn't even close to making you enough money to buy a new house. It will take you *years* to get there."

All these negative thoughts of lack and limitation and focusing on what I didn't have instead of what I did have were like weeds in my money garden, and they were strangling all my hopes and dreams of a better life for my family and me. I was stuck in default mode, and my mind kept gravitating toward the negative. I just kept thinking about how I didn't have enough money. I wasn't rich, so I'd never be able to afford my dream house, and it was impossible to move away from the prick next door.

I brooded about it for a *long* time and got myself so upset and agitated that I had to get out of the house and run it off. I ran hard and fast, and the bitterness started oozing out of my body. My thoughts started to loop on repeat: "You're not rich. You can't afford what you want. You're not rich." Tears started streaming down my face.

Then, suddenly, a new voice in my mind piped up. The voice said, "You're not walking your talk. You tell everybody to only hold in their minds what they want to experience. Are you saying that you don't want to be rich?"

Oh, damn! Guilty as charged! In that instant of awareness, I flipped the script. I replaced the scarcity thought and played, "I am rich, and I can afford whatever I want" on repeat instead. At first, it felt like a big, ol' fat lie. I had a serious internal conflict. Part of me was arguing that I wasn't rich and never would be, while another part of me was scrambling to find evidence to support that I was rich.

I shifted my mindset to abundance and started listing all the ways that I was rich. I was rich because I have my own business, and while it wasn't making as much money as I thought it should be (hello, unrealistic expectations!), it was making some money and gave me freedom and control in my life. I was rich because I had a wonderful family who loved me, pets I adored, and friends who would be there for me through anything. I was rich because I had talents and skills to offer to the world and because I was driven to work hard and succeed no matter what it took.

The list went on and on, and I kept repeating to myself, "I am rich now! I am rich now!" Because I had evidence to support the new belief, I really started to feel like I was rich. But I still had no idea how I was ever going to come up with the money for the farmhouse I wanted. I pushed on though, holding in my mind the belief that I would have it. It was mine.

I thought back to an intention I'd set almost a year prior to earn $125,000. It was mid-January 2017, and I'd just finished Napoleon Hill's book, *Think and Grow Rich*. It's a classic and worth adding to your reading list. The book had me thinking about money in a completely new way. Rather than seeing it as something of limited supply that was hard to obtain, I began seeing money as a resource that's as prevalent as the air I breathe. Money was all over the place, waiting to be transferred to me in all the right ways, at the right time, by the right people.

I started to believe that I deserved to have the money I wanted because I was working hard to be of service to others and add great value to the world. There was an exercise in the book that urged me to set an intention and ask the Universe to provide me with a specific amount of money by a certain date and then have firm faith and trust that the money would come to me, even if I couldn't see how it could possibly happen.

I thought it seemed a little ridiculous. I mean, the Universe wasn't just going to drop a bag full of money on my doorstep. I had nothing to lose by trying it, and if it worked, I'd be sold on the whole idea of attracting money with my mind. I thought long and hard about how much money I wanted, when I wanted to receive it, and the work I was willing to do in exchange for the money. I wrote it all out in my journal in the form of a prayer.

Here's the excerpt from my journal dated January 17, 2017:

"Universe, I am so grateful for the many blessings I receive each day: the warm sun on my face; a safe place to live; beautiful children to watch grow; a husband to love; fresh, clean water; and an abundance of food. Universe, I am looking to you as a partner in my business affairs for the guidance I need. I know I am led to see and do what is right, so I am supplied with money for every good need.

"I now declare that right contacts are established, right influences are set into motion, and right activities are started so that my abundance becomes manifest. I declare there is right action in all my affairs and that I give the best care to which I am capable, rendering the highest quality of service I can provide in all I do. I declare that earnings of $125,000 are rightfully mine, and I will have that amount in my possession by December 31, 2017.

"My faith is so strong; I can see the money before my eyes and touch it in my hands. I know the Universe responds to my believing word and that the right results and rewards are mine. I now go out and act accordingly. I express the attitude of abundance; I feel and look prosperous. I believe in my prosperity, and so I prosper.

"I await the transfer of the money belonging to me in the proportion that I deliver the service I intend to render for it. I am guided so that I see the right people, say and do the right things, give the right kind of service, and make myself valuable to others. Money to meet my every good requirement is now mine.

"I live wholesomely and efficiently and give generously. I am a good and faithful steward of this financial abundance. I am grateful for this abundant supply. I give sincere thanks for it, and it comes to me in exactly the right ways. I use this money freely in the service of God and humankind, knowing that as it goes out in every way and in loving helpfulness to others, it is constantly being blessed and that further money will take its place as quickly as needed."

I know, I know. It doesn't quite sound like my voice. That's because I was using Napoleon Hill's language as a template. The important part is that I intended to receive $125,000 by December 31, 2017. I had no freakin' idea how that was going to happen, but I read this prayer to myself every single day and believed it would all work out.

As I held the intention to attract this money into my life, money started showing up in various ways. My private practice got busier. We started working with insurance companies, and that generated more consistent income. Our clients started sharing our positive reputation around town and that brought in more paying clients.

But December 31, 2017 came and went, and I was far from making the $125,000 I asked for. However, at that point, I was so engrossed in running my business and enjoying the work I was doing that I didn't have time to question why I didn't receive the money I'd asked the Universe for. I just kept holding the intention in my mind without putting a deadline on it this time. I figured that sometimes projects take me longer to finish than expected, and maybe the Universe needed some extra time to bring that $125,000 to me, too. I just kept believing that the Universe was working behind the scenes to provide for me.

On June 30, 2018, exactly six months from the date I'd set to receive the money I wanted, we closed on the sale of the rental property we owned in Colorado and made $160,000 profit. The Universe provided $160,000 to me instead of $125,000! I figured the Universe was trying to make it up to me for the delay.

It was at that moment that I became an even stronger believer in the power of the mind, the power of the Universe, the value of asking specifically for what you want, and faith that you'll receive it, even if you can't see how it's possible. I thought the money would come from my business, but the Universe had different plans in mind. I thought it would come by the end of 2017, but the Universe delivered it right when I needed it. That money helped me get out of a stressful living situation and buy the little farm I'd dreamed of. That money helped me escape that miserable neighbor and made my dreams of acreage, a beautiful pool, and free-range chickens a reality. The advice I'd taken from that book was true. I received the money that was rightfully mine, in all the right ways, at exactly the right time from the right people.

Chapter 24

Attracting Money

I'm not an anomaly. I'm not special, and I don't consider myself to be a "lucky" person, which is how I know that this can work for you, too. In fact, there are countless examples of other people, all over the world, attracting money (and other desires) by setting intentions in their minds and recruiting the help of a higher power to manifest it. Real power exists in holding positive and affirming thoughts in your mind. Whatever you hold in your mind is created in reality. Whatever energy you send out to the Universe boomerangs back to you. Creating a prayer for what you hope to attract is an important spiritual practice that helps you stay focused on your intentions, without getting sidetracked, distracted, or discouraged.

Here are some of the elements that make up a powerful, wealth-attracting prayer:

- It is VERY specific.
- It is spoken from a place of gratitude and acceptance.

- It clearly indicates what you want to attract into your life.
- It declares "what is" (a.k.a. what you want life to be like and speaking of it as though it is that way now).
- It is spoken with absolute faith and trust that you will experience what you seek.

Try writing your own wealth-attracting prayer. I think you'll find it's an important tool for your ongoing spiritual practice and financial success. The other spiritual practice that I absolutely love is using mantras.

Mantras are short sayings that carry deep meaning and help you focus your attention on what you want to experience in life and your money relationship. Using mantras to attract your heart's desires into your life is also easy. All you have to do is write out short mantras and post them in places you'll see them frequently, like inside your planner, on the dashboard of your car, the refrigerator, or the bathroom mirror. These constant little reminders help you remember that there's a higher power working for you and the Universe is receiving your requests for money and busily working to bring it to you.

The Universe is your money maker. It creates new money every single day. All that money is yours for the taking if you want it. All you have to do to receive it is ask for it and have full faith and trust that all the money you seek will be transferred to you in exchange for the incredible value you offer to the world. That being said, we've already discussed the unfairness of society and how social injustices can widen the gap between where you are and where you want to be financially. I could write an entire book on that topic, but for now, let me just point out that while applying spiritual practices to attract more money into your life is simple, it isn't a cure-all. There will still be challenges and barriers to financial success that are outside of your control.

Below is a list of wealth-attracting mantras. You'll notice that these statements are written in the present tense, as though it is that way now. As part of your ongoing spiritual practice, state these mantras with absolute faith and trust that the Universe is providing you with your heart's desires NOW—not tomorrow, next month, or next year. As you speak these mantras to yourself or aloud, embrace the feeling that comes with experiencing your deepest desires in reality. Your thoughts become much more powerful when you attach a feeling to them.

State and feel at least one of these mantras each day:

- Money is a tool and a resource that enables me to live the life I want, and I welcome money into my life without feelings of guilt.
- The Universe is the constant giver of money for me. It replenishes my supply for every need I have.
- I focus my attention and my actions on the activities that I value most, and these result in financial prosperity.
- Monies are being transferred to me every day based on the quality and quantity of service I provide to others.
- I have a healthy relationship with money.
- I live honestly, efficiently, and generously, and as such, I am rewarded with an abundance of wealth.

- Every day, I am attracting and saving more and more money.
- I am creating true wealth in my life every day.
- Money is constantly flowing into my life, which allows me to live debt-free.
- I am always increasing my value to others, so I am always increasing the money I earn.
- I have a positive money mindset.
- I am grateful for the abundance I enjoy, and my attitude of gratitude attracts more wealth.
- Attracting money is easy and natural.
- God wants me to live the life of my dreams and offers me the money I need to live abundantly. I gladly and gratefully accept God's gifts.
- Money is good. Money is energy. Money is mine.
- I am fully supported in making money doing what I love to do.
- Money comes to me through various channels at various times for various services I provide.
- My earning potential is limitless. I openly welcome and accept all the abundance the Universe offers me.
- I am deserving of wealth and abundance.
- I am responsible with money. I attract money and manage it effectively.
- There is an abundance of money for everyone. I am rich, and my wealth does not take anything away from anyone else.
- Financial success and freedom are mine now.
- I appreciate and value money but am not attached to it. I let it freely flow in and out of my life, knowing that the Universe supplies me with more when it is needed.

These mantras can help you maintain a healthy relationship with your money and provide you with a sense of security and comfort that allows you to fully invest in your money relationship without fear. When you first start practicing these mantras, you might feel like you're lying to yourself. Fake it til you make it. With time, you'll come to believe these statements to be true. Keep looking for evidence to support that they are true now.

Chapter 25

Money Manifesto

I'm all about making things fun, especially money matters. If it's not fun, you won't want to do it. We've already established how important it is to tend to your finances and money relationship regularly, so the more fun and pleasure we can add to the mix, the better. As such, creating a money manifesto is a fun spin on writing a wealth-attracting prayer or using mantras, if neither of those practices is your jam. You could also integrate all three spiritual practices into your routine if you want to take your money-attracting power to the next level.

I'll be the first one to admit that it's ridiculously easy to get caught up in money drama. Stressing over paying all the bills on time, feeling like you have to "rob Peter to pay Paul" (borrowing money from one lender to pay the extending debt from another lender), worrying about all the debt hanging over your head, and feeling pressure to make more money so you can solve all your financial problems is a real emotional drag. Focusing on financial hardships can really eat up all your precious mental energy—energy that could be devoted to nurturing your money relationship.

More importantly, though, you don't really get to enjoy your life when you're all wrapped up in money stress. Financial stress affects absolutely every part of your life. It can negatively affect your relationships, self-esteem, physical and emotional health, sleep, and how you perform at work. Obesity. Smoking. Diabetes. These are the risk factors we typically think of when we consider threats to our overall health. We've all read about the dangers of maintaining a poor diet, putting carcinogenic substances into our bodies, and spending too much time on the couch binging on Netflix instead of sweating it out at the gym. But financial stress is a hidden danger that poses an even greater risk to our health and well-being.

The toll that financial stress takes on our lives and overall health is often overlooked. After all, everyone has money problems, right? And because most people have complicated feelings about money (like guilt, shame, anxiety, and overwhelm), they often avoid tending to their finances because it's just too much to deal with. So, why are we so stressed out about money?

A 2017 report in *MarketWatch* found that fifty percent of Americans live paycheck-to-paycheck and almost twenty percent of people have no savings to speak of. On surveys, people report feeling anxious and fearful about their financial well-being and "struggling to make ends meet," even if they're making six-figure incomes. Then, a pandemic swept across the globe and caused an even bigger financial crisis. No wonder we lay awake at night worrying about how to pay the bills and find ourselves crying over our empty bank accounts.

The consequences of overspending and underearning don't just affect our wallets. Our mental, emotional, and physical health suffers too. Financial stress can cause a number of issues, including:

- Sleep issues and insomnia
- Increased likelihood of illness
- Headaches
- Muscle/Joint aches and pains
- Cardiovascular disease
- Mood issues
- Relationship issues
- Absences from work
- Substance abuse
- Clinical depression and anxiety

As a licensed psychotherapist, you think I'd know how to ward off depression, anxiety, and major money fights with my husband, but financial stress doesn't discriminate. Several years ago, I found myself in the same position as many of my clients: in the midst of a financial hot mess; constantly on edge; and unable to get the fear of bankruptcy, divorce, and losing my business out of my head. During my financial dark days, I fought with my husband about money almost daily. I was snippy and impatient with my children. Emotionally, I was like a tea kettle building with steam. At any given moment, my top would suddenly blow off, and I'd erupt in anger. When my husband would casually inquire about when I would ever bring home a paycheck from my business, I'd bite his head off in defensiveness, which would turn into hour-long fights about money.

My feelings of desperation and financial chaos led to angry outbursts, feelings of guilt and shame, low self-esteem, depression, anxiety, and hopelessness. The financial stress I experienced affected every area of my life, including how I performed at work, how I interacted with the people I loved, and how my body functioned. (I'll spare you the gross details of the intestinal issues, chronic acne, and "unexplained" weight loss I went through.)

Worrying about money is exhausting. Life shouldn't be all about money and trying to figure out how to make ends meet. Life is really about having the time and freedom to be with the people you love. It's about doing meaningful work that lights you up and getting compensated for that work with a crush-worthy salary. It's about being present and happy, experiencing life's guilty pleasures, learning and growth, sex, and hot vanilla lattes. It's about laughing with your kids, playing board games for hours, and creating works of art (whether they make you money or not).

Interestingly, these are the reasons we all want money. Money is awesome because it makes it easier to have the lifestyle you truly want. Making the kind of money you desire, managing your money effectively and with confidence, working toward financial independence, and using your money as a tool to have and do everything you want in life is a **financial lifestyle**. If you want to create a financial lifestyle you're totally obsessed with, one that makes your heart skip a beat and has you crushing so hard on your money, you have to talk the talk and walk the walk.

Creating a money manifesto is the way to do this. Your money manifesto is your ideal financial lifestyle written out in black and white so you can reference it regularly. It helps you to make sure you're living your best financial life, one step at a time, every single day. Your money manifesto is a testament to what's most important to you, what you care about, what you stand for, what you want to do with your money, and how you want to live your life. In short, your money manifesto isn't just about dollars and cents. It's about living the life you want. That's what money is about, too. It is the resource or the tool that makes living the life you want possible.

Let me share my money manifesto with you so you can see what I mean:

"In my world, weekly money dates spent tweaking my spending plan and sipping hot, vanilla, almond-milk lattes is a complete guilty pleasure. Slowly caressing soft fabrics at Marshalls, looking for my next inexpensive impulse buy, is always a fabulous idea. Social media is overrated and spending more than thirty minutes a day on Facebook or Instagram is not an option. Saying 'YES!' feels like jumping out of bed at 6:30 a.m. for daily journaling with a side of piping hot coffee (spiked with a dose of collagen to keep that youthful glow) and fuzzy snuggles from my cat, Mowgli. Saying 'NO!' feels like honoring myself with the promise and commitment to create the work I'm put on this earth to do without getting sidetracked or distracted by someone else's goals. I care deeply about empowering women to take an active role in their financial lives, to unapologetically earn as much money as they want, and to manage their money with confidence and excitement. I believe that using your money as a tool to spend less time at the office and more time with the people you love is crush-worthy. Morning jogs with the dog, coffee dates with girlfriends, day sex when the kids aren't home, and spontaneous '90s pop dance parties with my daughters are non-negotiable. Giving generously to people and animals in need and using my money as an unstoppable force for good in the world is an absolute necessity. Fantasizing about spending countless hours writing self-help books in quaint coffee shops all over the world is totally reasonable. Striving for a simple, slow, joyful life full of presence and gratitude is a must. Keeping up with the Joneses, comparing myself to others, and buying into the idea that 'more is better' is an absolute 'NO.' And at the end of the day, knowing I did my best to be of service to others while staying true to myself is all that really matters."

Now, it's your turn. Schedule an hour-long money date this week, and use that time to work on creating your own money manifesto. Use my manifesto as a template, or create your own beautiful masterpiece! Get specific about what you want to do, how you want to feel, and the kind of lifestyle you want your money to support. Ask the Universe for help. Lean into the incredible connection you have to the Universe to make all your money dreams realities!

Money Therapy Assignment

Money Manifesto: create a testament of what's most important to you, what you care about, what you stand for, what you want to do with your money, and how you want to live your life so you can work toward that vision every day

Using the template below, fill in the blanks and write out your money manifesto. Let this be a living, breathing document that changes over time as your financial life changes. Hold these intentions in your mind every day so you can mindfully live in alignment with these intentions. Not only will your money manifesto connect you to a higher power, but it will also connect you to the deepest, most genuine parts of yourself.

In my world, _____ and _____ are complete guilty pleasures.

_____, _____, or _____ is always a fabulous idea.

_____ is overrated, and _____ is not an option.

Saying "YES!" feels like _____ and _____.

Saying "NO!" feels like _____.

I care deeply about _____, _____, and _____.

I believe that using your money as a tool to spend time_____ is crush-worthy.

_____, _____, _____, and _____ are non-negotiable.

Giving generously to _____ and using my money for _____ is an absolute necessity.

Fantasizing about _____ is totally reasonable.

Striving for a _____, _____, _____ life full of _____ and _____ is a must.

_____, _____, and _____ is an absolute "NO."

And at the end of the day, _____ is all that really matters.

Take a moment to bask in the glow of all the good vibes that come from knowing that for every step you take toward your financial goals, the Universe is taking 10,000 steps on your behalf. Then, brace yourself. We're about to examine the dark side of the money relationship.

PART VII: MAKE UP OR BREAK UP

Chapter 26

Make Up or Break Up

Once you've been in any type of relationship for a while, you sorta stop seeing all the positive features in that person and begin to hone in on the negative aspects of them. The rose-colored glasses come off, and you find yourself getting irritated and annoyed by all the weird idiosyncrasies your partner seems to have. I've seen it a hundred times (and have been guilty of it myself). Couples navigate out of the romance stage and into the conflict stage of the relationship. I call this the "make-up or break-up stage" because the way a couple deals with their differences ultimately determines whether they will stay together or part ways. This is the stage when most couples come to me for help.

If you've ever been in couple's therapy, you already know that it's not always pretty. There's an ugly side to the process. Over my twenty-year career doing this work, I've had a lot of therapy sessions go bad. As you can imagine, the therapist's office is (by design) a safe, judgment-free zone for couples to explore their most private thoughts and feelings with each other. Couples take full advantage of this safe space. They often use it as the place to reveal secrets they've been keeping for years or admit to the lies they've been telling their partner.

I remember one couple who decided my office was the best place to reveal the lies they'd been keeping from each other for years. Candace was complaining about how distant Dave was acting. She noted that he seemed so detached from her like he'd rather be anywhere else than with her. Dave had been making excuses about this for weeks. His job took a lot out of him, and he just didn't have any energy when he got home. He was distracted with worry about his brother, who was struggling with a gambling addiction. He didn't feel like he was getting enough time to himself to blow off steam.

These seemed like reasonable explanations for his distance, but Candace wasn't buying it. She kept pushing and prodding to get the *real* reason why Dave seemed disinterested in her. It was actually starting to annoy me. I thought to myself, *Back the hell off, Candace. Dave is doing his best.* As a therapist, I have to keep my opinions to myself and act as a neutral party who advocates for the best interests of the relationship. So, I kept my mouth shut and waited to see how this dynamic would unfold.

Finally, after weeks of Candace badgering Dave about being distant, he lost it. "Fine! Do you want to know the truth? I'll tell you the truth! You gained fifty pounds when you got pregnant, and you haven't lost the weight yet. It's been four years! I'm just not physically attracted to you anymore because of that. So, I avoid you because I don't want you to try to have sex with me."

Ouch. I bet you can guess how Candace reacted to Dave's confession. When the truth comes out, the gloves come off. As the innocent bystander in it all, I've often been caught in the crosshairs of screaming matches, put in the middle of entangled relationship messes, and left alone in my office as one or both of my clients storm out in frustration.

How could I blame Candace for storming out, feeling hurt and frustrated? When things get intense and heated, some clients just want to get the hell outta there! Not gonna lie; there have been times I've wanted to run out of my office screaming, too. Needless to say, these emotional outbursts, verbal WWE matches, and attacks at each other's soft spots aren't helpful in healing the relationship. I see the same dynamic playing out in money relationships.

Chapter 27

Bullying Your Money

When the passion of the romance stage wears off, couples start seeing the worst in each other. They begin jumping to conclusions and making assumptions about their partner, perceiving each other more negatively than they should. The cute, endearing quirks they admired about each other at the beginning of the relationship become viewed as faults and flaws.

I used to love how my husband would snuggle up to me in the middle of the night. Now? When he creeps over to my side of the bed and wraps his whole body around mine, suffocating me in a burning cocoon of body heat, I want to sucker punch him in the face. When we start assuming that our partner's behavior is done deliberately to annoy us, or because they have no consideration for our feelings, or interpret the irritating behaviors as a sign that our partner doesn't really love us, we feel resentful toward our partner. So resentful that we start blaming them for all of our unhappiness. Just ask my husband, and he'll confirm this is true.

Once you've been in any type of relationship for a while, you become keenly aware of all your partner's weird quirks, and they start to drive you bananas.

"OMG, why does he have to chew so loud?"

"If she leaves a dirty dish sitting *beside* the sink instead of *in* it one more time, I'm going to lose my shit!"

"Replacing the roll of toilet paper does not cause brain damage! What's his problem?"

You've probably caught yourself thinking similar things about your current or former romantic partner, and whether you know it or not, you do the same exact thing with your money. The problem with perceiving your money in negative ways is that it colors your entire relationship, just like one little drop of ink colors the entire glass of water.

Before you know it, you're blaming your money for all your problems. You feel like a victim of your circumstances and that it's all your money's fault. This makes you distrust your money, and you certainly aren't swooning over it. If you're constantly feeling irritated and annoyed by your money, you're going to be grumpy toward it. You'll call it names. Talk smack about it. Be careful, or your money will retaliate. Then, we've got a real money drama on our hands.

A frequent problem I see in my work as a financial therapist is that women talk smack about their money, and then it doesn't want to be around them. I bet you do this, too. Does hearing me say that make you cringe and want to defend yourself? Are you now thinking, "That's not at all true! I don't talk smack about my money!" Well, let's find out.

Have you ever said anything (to yourself or aloud) like this:

"Money is the root of all evil."
"Money is a personal thing and talking about it is so rude and inappropriate."
"There's never enough money."
"I can't have what I want because I can't afford it."
"It's greedy and selfish to want more money."
"I can't ask for THAT MUCH money. They'll laugh in my face."
"So what if I'm not making that much money? I don't need money anyway!"

It's okay to admit that you've been talking smack. I promise you won't get grounded for it. But it's important that you own the fact that you've been kind of mean to your money and understand that when you bully your money, it doesn't want to be around you. If your money has hightailed it out of your life or seems to be ghosting you, it just might be because you're not talking very nicely to it or about it. You know that old saying, "Sticks and stones can break my bones, but words will never hurt me"? When it comes to talking smack about your money, words absolutely can hurt your money and you.

Thinking about money as being something evil, off-limits, or never there when you need it keeps you from having it because when you don't respect your money or treat it with kindness, it moves on to someone who will shower it with the praise and the admiration it deserves. The negative internal dialogue plays on repeat—all day, every day—

and you might not even be aware that you're talking badly about your money in your own mind.

The negative words that get flung around in your head corrupt the money relationship because the words that you use to describe your money influence how you feel about it. Your feelings about money influence how you behave with it. The way you talk about money with other people affects your relationship with money, too.

Do you chronically complain to everyone you know that you're so broke? Are your friends always inviting you to do fun things with them only to hear you say, "No, I can't afford it"? Are you often gossiping with your girlfriends about all the things you want but can't have because there's never enough money to go around? All of these thoughts are grounded in scarcity, and scarcity begets more scarcity.

If your partner was constantly telling everyone all about how you're never there for them, you never do enough, they can't count on you, and you don't meet their needs, would you want to hang out with your partner? Would you even dream of spending time with someone who talked about you like that? Fuck no. Your money feels the very same way.

I know how hard it can be to flip the script and start thinking about money in a more positive light. There was a time when I could have been the poster child for money bullying. I was always told that if you don't have anything nice to say, don't say anything at all. I live by that rule of thumb. When it came to money though, that advice got chucked out the window. I would find myself saying things like, "Money sucks. It's never around when I need it." "Ugh! I can't afford the things I want! There's not enough money!"

I remember one time, I wanted to take a day off from work to visit my best friend in Washington, D.C., but when

I looked at my bank account, I knew I couldn't swing it. I couldn't afford to miss a day of work and lose that income. I couldn't afford the gas to get there. I couldn't afford to eat out all weekend. I couldn't go because of money. I was pissed. My thoughts were ugly. *Money really is the root of all evil. I fucking hate how money controls my life. Why do other people have so much money, and I'm struggling to get by? What gives?* Smack-talking money was a daily occurrence. No wonder money ran away and hid from me. I was bullying my money. Putting it down. Calling it names and blaming it for all the problems in my life.

Money bolts when disrespected like that. It's not going to stick around to be trash-talked. When money dropped me like it's hot, I cried into my coffee (more times than I like to admit). Then, I became determined to figure out where I'd gone wrong. Putting on my couple's therapist cap, I thought about all the hostile conversations I'd observed in my office. I looked back at the "conversations" I'd had with my money and realized how tragic and pathetic they were. I realized that I'd been such a total jerk to my money. I made a vow to apply the "say something nice or nothing at all" rule to my money.

I then started loving up on my money to make up for all the hurtful things I'd said to it in the past. In my mind, I tried to make the dialogue flirty. I thought about the way my husband and I would text each other during the day when we first started dating and used that as a template for how I wanted to speak to my money.

"Money, you're so dreamy. You're always doing things for me and making my life easier. I can always count on you to be there when I need you. When I see you come into my bank account, my heart starts beating faster. I can't wait to experience all the things we'll do together!"

I know. It sounds so cheesy, right? But it works for two reasons. First, it gets you laughing at yourself and adds lightness and comedy to your financial situation. If you don't laugh, you'll cry. And haven't you done enough of that already? Secondly, when you start thinking about money in a more compassionate, fun, playful way, you start feeling that way about money. The good vibes alleviate the emotional pressure and help you see new solutions to old financial problems. It frees you up to think more objectively about your finances and envision options you may not have seen before.

When I stopped being a bully and started being a good girlfriend to my money, it came around more often and stayed around longer. The revenue in my business increased five times in just eight months, and new clients kept calling to book appointments with me. Since I wasn't so worried and scared about my income, I finally had the mental capacity to examine my expenses and reduce them. Cutting costs that weren't essential or didn't generate more revenue kept more money in my pocket. After a while, I was able to save more and earn interest on those savings, making even more money.

Before I knew it, my money and I had a steamy little love affair going. Yet, had I not gone through Money Therapy[R] and started talking nice to my money, I would still be in the same broke-ass place I was back then. Ask yourself: Are you being a bully to your money? Do you find yourself talking smack about it while still expecting it to hang out with you? If so, you and your money need to have a seat on the therapist's couch. You're now in Money Therapy[R].

Chapter 28

Money Therapy

Most couples wait far too long to come to therapy. Instead of being proactive and seeking help when problems first begin, they wait until there's a full-blown crisis. This is how most people deal with money problems too, and why it's time to bite the bullet and do Money Therapy^R now before a real financial disaster strikes (if it hasn't already).

What exactly is Money Therapy^R? Well, you've been doing it since you started reading this book. Here's a more formal definition for nerdy, brainiacs like me: Money Therapy^R is the process by which psychological theories and interventions are used to solve problems and improve the relationship with money. It's a process by which you heal your relationship with money, gain financial confidence, and learn how to manage your money strategically. Money Therapy^R gets you in the habit of taking an active role in your financial life, enhances your financial literacy, and helps you make informed financial decisions. In short, Money Therapy^R changes the way you think, feel, and behave with money.

Just like couple's therapy, Money Therapy^R can get messy. Sometimes your finances can feel like *Fight Club*. Do you remember that movie? It's one of my favorite psychological dramas. What's not to love about a materialistic insomniac who starts a secret underground club (with very strict rules) for men who want to spice up their mundane lives by fighting each other? Before the main character in the film (who remains nameless throughout) starts *Fight Club*, he spends his days in a tedious job he hates and his nights shopping for home furnishings to make the perfect apartment. He spends a ton of money buying a ton of stuff (hello, retail therapy), but he's still depressed and bored.

Then he meets Tyler Durden (who we later find out is the main character's alter ego), and when they team up to start *Fight Club*, there is all sorts of action in his life. But he can't talk about it to anyone because the first rule of *Fight Club* is "Don't talk about *Fight Club*." All the guys in the club show up to work with black eyes and battle scars, but no one would ever dare tell the truth about how they got them. They all made up stories to keep *Fight Club* a big ol' secret, which is what I used to do with money.

Just like in *Fight Club*, I used to show up in life with financial bruises and scars from my fights with money. I'd find myself coming up with all sorts of stories and lies instead of fessing up to what was really going on financially. People would ask me how my business was going, and I'd lie and say it was great so I wouldn't have to face the guilt and shame of admitting my business was losing money every day.

In my mind, I'd play the victim and blame money for messing up my whole life and "forcing" me to lie like that. I kept my money fights a secret from my husband so he wouldn't freak out about me not being able to pay us anything that month. My experience working with couples like Candace and Dave taught me that secret-keeping posed the greatest threat to a relationship. Secrets and lies create a slippery slope that can lead to bad decisions; decisions that have the potential to destroy the relationship. I realized that not talking honestly about money was like playing with fire, and the moment I made that discovery was just like the moment in the movie when the main character realizes he has dissociative identity disorder. I felt like the world was swirling around me, and all my money memories flashed before my eyes.

I didn't want anything coming between me and my money or me and my husband, Tom. Not fights, secrets, or lies. Finally, I worked up the nerve and came clean to my husband about our financial mess. Talking to Tom about our financial dumpster fire was like ripping off a BAND-AID. I could confess slowly over time and feel every little sting and pull, or I could just do it all at once and get it over with. I went for it and confessed everything. It was devastating to admit that we were in so much debt and tell him that the business I was so sure would be successful wasn't doing well. I hated admitting that I still couldn't put any money toward the monthly bills. There were a lot of tears, questions, and raised voices. It was very similar to the way Candace and Dave responded to each other when Dave finally came clean about his true feelings.

I felt like such a failure. I felt sorry for Tom for being married to such a loser who couldn't run a business worth shit, let alone bring home some money for groceries. I felt overcome with guilt for hiding our dire financial circumstances from him for so long and ashamed that I kept pouring money into getting my business off the ground, making Tom work longer hours to compensate for the money I was spending.

Intense situations (like conversations about money, infidelity, or lying) can make it easy for the therapy session to get out of control. After too many therapy sessions had gone wrong, I knew I needed to develop a framework that would create structure for the session and guide couples through the therapeutic process smoothly and more productively. I call it the "restructuring frustrations framework." By establishing some ground rules and applying this framework to every therapy session, I was able to reduce negative interactions and increase productive problem-solving and empathetic discussion.

Since it works so well in couple's therapy, I decided to apply it to my money relationship. The framework very quickly became an important part of the Money Therapy^R process because it worked wonders for my relationship with money. I'm certain it will work for you and your money as well.

Chapter 29

Restructuring Frustrations

Feelings of frustration toward your money are inevitable. You can't prevent them from coming up. What you can control is how you respond to those frustrations, and that makes all the difference in your money relationship. Instead of spewing your anger and frustration all over the place and hurting your money's feelings, you need to restructure these frustrations so you and your money can work together productively to overcome them.

The restructuring frustrations framework consists of 6 steps:

Step 1: Get clear about what's really bothering you.
Sometimes we know we're upset, but we don't really know why or what's causing the negative feelings. The first thing to do is figure out what's frustrating you when it

comes to your financial situation. Write it out. "What frustrates me about my financial situation is _____."

Step 2: Identify your feelings.
Now that you know what's bothering you, figure out how that makes you feel. Write out your feelings for each frustration point. It might sound something like this: "What frustrates me about my financial situation is that I have $50,000 in student loans. I don't know how I'll ever get rid of them. I feel scared and overwhelmed about this."

Step 3: Identify how you behave in response to these thoughts and feelings.
You might not yet be aware of how your behavior is driven by the way you feel about your money. You might be acting on autopilot and not really paying attention to the unhelpful behaviors that are actually making your financial situation worse. In this step, examine what you do as a result of how you feel about your financial situation, like this: "What I actually do because of feeling scared and overwhelmed is I only pay the minimum on my student loans and don't even attempt to pay them off early."

Step 4: Identify your hidden fear.
Our underlying and unconscious fears are the primary motivators for our behavior. Not sure why you're acting like you do? I bet fear is at the root of it. Dive deep and figure out what your hidden fear is, because your behavior is an attempt to hide that fear so it can't be detected by you or anyone else. A hidden fear might look something like: "I avoid paying extra on my student loans to hide my fear

that I'll never be able to pay them off and will never truly be financially free."

Step 5: Identify your hidden desires.
A secondary motivator for our behavior is desire. Now you need to get clear on what it is that you want, or you'll never get it. What do you desire from your money? What could your money do that would make your frustration over your financial situation disappear? It might sound similar to this: "What I desire from my money is to make enough of it that I can pay off my student loans in under two years, save money on the interest I'm currently paying, and finally feel like I'm gaining financial traction."

Step 6: Map out the steps you need to take with your money to obtain your desires.
You are *not* a victim of your circumstances! Your money is *not* working against you! In this final step of the framework, outline concrete action steps for how you and your money can work together to achieve the desired goal, such as: "To obtain my desire to pay off my student loan in under two years, my money and I need to have a money date every week and use that time to look for ways to reduce expenses and put the difference toward paying extra toward the student loans."

By moving through each step of this framework, you'll realize that you are in control of your thoughts, feelings, and behaviors. You get to choose how you feel about your money, how you behave with your money, and what happens in your financial life. You have the power to transform frustrations, irritations, and annoyance toward your money into action, appreciation, and love for your money and what it can do for you. Now, let's put everything you've learned into practice.

Money Therapy Assignment

Restructuring Frustrations-identifying specific frustrations with money; the feelings, fears, behaviors, and desires you experience as a result of those frustrations; and how to obtain your desires from money in better ways.

Schedule a money date this week and devote your time to working through each step of the restructuring frustrations framework described in this chapter. Then complete this exercise to get you in the habit of giving your money the benefit of the doubt.

1. Fold a piece of lined paper in half. On one side of the paper, write down three things that your money does that you dislike, drives you crazy, or you just cannot stand.

Here are some common examples:

- My money never seems to be there for me.
- I just can't stand how my (lack of) money makes me feel unsuccessful and like a huge failure.
- It drives me nuts when my money disappears right after payday and there's nothing left over to have fun with.
- My money is all work and no play these days. Ugh!

2. Next, flip the paper over, and for each of the negative things/complaints, write five positive qualities that you cherish, love, and/or appreciate about your money.

Here are some common examples:

- I love how my money finds ways to cheer me up and show me it loves me by treating me to vanilla lattes at Starbucks each week.
- I cherish how my money made it possible for me to take a week-long vacation with my family to Jamaica.
- I appreciate my money for always being there to pay the electric bill, so I don't have to worry about getting caught in the dark or losing a week's worth of groceries.

3. Finally, rip the paper in half and throw away the negative side. Review the remaining positive qualities every day this week.

PART VIII: THREATS TO THE MONEY RELATIONSHIP

Chapter 30

Potential Threats to Your Money Relationship

I wish I could tell you that restructuring frustrations and spending quality time with your money would solve all your money relationship problems and send you two riding off into the sunset together, but that's not how relationships work. There are ups and downs in every relationship and potential threats that could leave you sleeping on the couch (or lying there awake, worrying about money).

When Brad Pitt and Angelina Jolie costarred in *Mr. & Mrs. Smith*, a serious threat popped up for Jennifer Aniston. Jen wanted to stay focused on her career. Brad wanted to start a family. They weren't seeing eye to eye.

Then in walks Angelina in all her sexy, full-lipped glory, right into a sex scene with Brad. Disaster was written all over it! Jen didn't have a chance! Angelina promised Brad to bear his children, and the rest was history! Had the relationship between Brad and Jen been super tight, maybe the outcome would have been different. But when a relationship is struggling and a potential threat comes along, it's damn near impossible to protect it from catastrophe.

MONEY TRUTH: You have to *proactively* be on the lookout for potential threats to your money relationship and head them off fast.

You don't want your money relationship to come to a screeching halt or lose your money to someone else. No way! You gotta safeguard your money relationship from these common threats:

Threat #1: Cheating

Anytime you blow your spending plan by splurging on random things you didn't budget for, you're cheating on your money. Remember how consumerism and neuromarketing actively manipulate your buying habits? Consumerism and neuromarketing seduce you into straying from your committed money relationship!

Consumerism and neuromarketing lure you, tempt you, and promise to make you feel oh-so-good, but if you give in to their manipulation, the infidelity will destroy the relationship with your money. Cheating is generally considered the ultimate betrayal, and one of the most difficult issues to bounce back from in a relationship. This is because trust is so critical. It's the foundation a relationship is built on. If there's no trust, the relationship remains vulnerable to a variety of potential threats that can destroy the relationship. Not only that, but you'll also feel terrible in the relationship. Rather than feeling loved and adored, safe, comfortable, flirty, and fun, you'll feel scared, irritable, defensive, suspicious, confused, contemptuous, and maybe even withdrawn.

To be head-over-heels in love with your money and build a strong foundation for your relationship to grow, you need to get to the bottom of what's really going on and figure out if any cheating is happening in your money relationship. Notice I didn't say that you need to figure out if your money is *cheating on you*. I said, "*if any cheating*" is happening. That includes a thorough investigation of the money relationship to see if you are cheating on your money. It works both ways, you know. Before you get all defensive and be like, "I ain't no cheater," keep in mind that you might be cheating on your money and not even realize you're doing it. When it comes to cheating, what should you be looking for? How can you tell if someone is cheating in the relationship?

Here are 7 signs of financial infidelity:

1. There's been a lot more spending than usual.

Random charges on your bank statement. Numerous visits to Target in the same week. An inbox full of Paypal receipts. A dwindling account balance. You might be able to blame this on your money if you're the victim of identity theft and someone else is blowing your cash. But if you're the one spending here, there, and everywhere, then you're the cheater in this situation.

2. It's all about appearances.

The focus is no longer on paying off debt, saving for the future, paying for your kids to go to college, or using your money to make an impact on the world. It's about looking good and impressing people.

Maybe it comes in the form of spending a ton of dough on beauty rituals for yourself, like cuts and colors every six weeks, gel nails, false eyelashes, designer clothes, and MAC makeup (in every color palette). Or maybe it's fancy furniture for your living room, a new Lexus in your driveway, and an addition to the master bedroom (because there ain't no way Karen is going to have a bigger bedroom than you!). This is a sign that values have gone out the window, and someone (probably you) is "chasing tail."

3. Intimacy is avoided.

Your money doesn't want to be with you, and you don't want to be with your money. Displays of love, appreciation, admiration, and affection are nonexistent. Money dates are so not happening ever. You can't even remember the last time you had one. And you don't really want to have one either because you feel contempt for your money. You're feeling negative toward it, and you'd rather avoid it than deal with the complicated feelings you have about it. Since love and passion aren't part of your money relationship right now, there's a chance that you or your money might be looking for love someplace else.

4. There's a sudden need for more privacy.

You used to be open and honest with your money, having money dates to check in and see what your money's been up to. You also used to be honest and transparent about your money with your partner, discussing the details of your financial lives and working together as a team to gain financial power. If there's a sudden need for more privacy and you find yourself keeping secrets and hiding the details of what's going on with your money, cheating might be at play. Healthy relationships are about openness and transparency. If there's any secrecy happening, it's a huge red flag that something's amiss.

5. More fights are being picked.

If you start feeling angry with your money all the time and you don't know why, it could be because you feel bad about how you're treating it and you want to turn your money into the bad guy to alleviate your own guilt. Are you being hypercritical of your cash? Nitpicking about every little thing that irritates you about your current financial situation? It might be because you're cheating on your money or you're mistreating it and you're looking for a reason to be pissed at it to justify misusing it.

6. Major money mood swings start happening.

A person who's cheating is likely to have rapidly shifting moods because the wild ups and downs of having an affair create excitement, but also confusion, guilt, and uncertainty about what will happen next. It's kinda like when you go shopping. When you're in the middle of it, it feels thrilling, satisfying, and blissful. Then when you get home, unpack your bags, and deduct the amount you spent from your budget, the letdown sets in. Feelings of guilt and shame pop up. One minute you were happy. The next, you're somber and depressed. If you find yourself loving your money and what it can do for you one minute and then hating, resenting, and fearing your money the next, chances are pretty good that you're not being a faithful girlfriend to your cash.

7. You get overly defensive when someone asks you about money.

Your partner asks you how much you spent on eating out last week. Your accountant asks you what your business expenses were for the year and why they've gone up since last year. Your girlfriends want to know if you got the raise you've been talking about for the past three months. (You haven't.) All these innocent questions make you want to rip their heads off, then crawl under the covers and never, ever talk about (or think about) money again.

"It's none of their business! I shouldn't have to explain myself or account for every single penny I spend! Who cares if I didn't get a raise? Those jerks couldn't spot true talent from a mile away!" Defensiveness is incredibly common when there's cheating going on because if someone starts asking questions that imply you're being unfaithful to your money, you're probably going to *deny* it.

Threat #2: Blame

You already know that blaming your money for all your problems and expecting it to fix things for you creates negative feelings—like anger, fear, resentment, and hatred toward your money—that undermine the relationship. Pointing fingers at yourself and labeling yourself as a terrible partner to your money, financially irresponsible, or bad with money does your relationship no good either. There doesn't need to be a "bad guy" in the situation. If you're spending a lot of time and energy trying to figure out who's to blame, you're inviting this potential threat to take over your love affair with money and crush it.

Threat #3: Keeping Up with the Joneses

Chronically comparing yourself to others and spending a boatload of money trying to keep up with people you aspire to be like is a huge threat to your money relationship. You and your money have plans with each other that are more important than impressing people. You want to actually be rich, not just look like you are. Be careful to protect your long-term financial goals from the impulse to be "like everybody else."

Threat #4: Secrets and Lies

When things with your money aren't going great, you might be tempted to leave out some details, stretch the truth, or tell a little white lie. When people who care about you inquire about your financial health, it can be painful to tell the truth: You're not making the kind of money you want yet, or you're drowning in debt. But trust me, it's way less painful to be honest than it is to undo the damage that's caused by deceit and lies. If it's a romantic partner you're lying to, he/she/they will find out the truth eventually and dishonesty will cause him/her/them to feel like you're not reliable or consistent. Your partner might start fearing that you may take advantage of them or that you're lying about other things too.

Threat #5: Fighting Unfairly

You and your money are bound to have disagreements. You might think that the interest rate on your investment account should be 12% while your money (a.k.a. the stock market) is saying it can only be 8% right now. In instances of conflict, fighting isn't necessarily a bad thing. It's just a form of communication (and communication is a good thing). You have to *fight fair* with your money. No name-calling. No blaming. No cheating on your money to make yourself feel better about the fight. No impulsive behavior like withdrawing all the funds in your portfolio because the market is down that day.

Chapter 31

Use Protection

The last thing you want is for you and your money to have heated battles that ultimately lead to a messy break-up and arguing over who gets to keep Sparky. That's why you're here. You want to cure money relationship problems and make your money relationship work. If you want your love affair with money to last a lifetime, you have to guard it with your life. Not in the possessive, hoarding-all-your-money way, but in the proactive, take-good-care-of-your-money way. In the previous chapter, you learned about some of the potential threats to your money relationship. Now, here's the skinny on how to protect your money relationship from each of those threats (cheating, blame, keeping up with the Joneses, secrets & lies, and fighting unfairly):

1. Keep your money dates.

Dust off your spending plan (more on this later). Frequently remind yourself of your short- and long-term goals with your money. Stay committed to those goals. When consumerism and neuromarketing show up all hot and sexy, give 'em the cold shoulder. You don't need retail therapy or a hit of dopamine to make you feel good anymore. You've got your money honey to keep you cozy at night.

2. Let go of blame and anger

If you've been carrying around anger, blame, resentment, and frustration toward your money, now is the time to let that shit go. In every moment up until now, your money has been doing the best it could, given the circumstances, and so have you. Stop blaming your money or yourself, and recognize that you and your money have turned over a new leaf by being in Money Therapy^R together. Trust the therapeutic process and have confidence that the deep inner work you're doing in Money Therapy^R is setting the course for financial success. Let go of the past and quit dwelling on it so it doesn't corrode your current money relationship.

3. Keep Your Eyes on Your Own Paper

Quit paying so much attention to what everyone else is doing and buying. You do you, boo. You don't need all the fancy, shiny things. You don't have to be like everybody else. (Honestly, who would want to be?) Focus more on your money relationship and nurturing it with money dates than you do on shopping, impressing people, and trying to keep up with all the latest whatevers.

4. Be Open & Honest

Be honest with yourself about how you're thinking, feeling, and behaving with your money, even if you don't like what you see. Keep having regular money dates where you examine the current state of your finances. Doing so will help you gain awareness about what's happening, what's working well, and what needs to change. Be open with your partner, even if it's scary. Be honest with other people when you're talking about money. It takes way less energy to be genuine, authentic, and honest than it does to put on a show, keep secrets, and cover up lies.

5. Fight Fair

If a problem comes up with your money (like going over your spending plan limit for the month, a dip in the stock market, or making a financial decision you end up regretting), don't freak out. Don't act impulsively. Definitely don't do something drastic like crumpling up your spending plan, pulling all your investments out, or maxing out your credit card. Take a big, deep breath and do this instead:

- **Clearly identify the problem.** ("My car broke down this month, and now I'm $1,000 over budget.")
- **Explore what's contributing to that money issue.** ("I haven't been setting aside money in an emergency fund to cover unexpected expenses. Because of that, I had to put the car repairs on a credit card, which derails my goals for paying off debt.")
- **Calmly brainstorm ideas of how you can improve/solve the problem.** ("I can pay off the credit card balance as quickly as possible to avoid paying interest. Then, I can put $100 in an emergency fund each month, so I'll be prepared the next time a big expense comes up.")

Thank your money for always being willing to work with you on financial problems like these. ("Thanks for being there with me through all the ups and downs and working with me to figure all this money stuff out!")

Chapter 32

Expectations and Agreements

There's one more threat to the money relationship that you have to be on the lookout for: having unreasonable expectations about what your money can and will do for you. At one point, I expected my money to buy me a Louis Vuitton bag, fly me to Los Angeles to see Katy Perry in concert, pay off my Mastercard, and renovate my master bathroom all in the same year, but that didn't mean my money was willing and able to do all that. Before you go assuming that your money is going to jump when you ask it to, you need to sit down with your money and see if it's willing and able to give you what you want. If it can't, you need to be flexible and figure out a different plan.

What do you think happens when your money doesn't meet your expectations? How do you respond when you don't get what you want when you want it? Expectations are the ideas you hold in your mind about how things should be. Agreements involve communicating your expectations with your partner/money to see if they are willing and able to meet them and negotiating a compromise until a mutually beneficial arrangement can be reached.

Now, look back at the definition for expectations and notice the word "should." This is a terrible, dangerous, drama-creating, disappointment-breeding word, and it needs to be banned from your vocabulary for life. When you use the word "should," you're basically trying to motivate yourself to do things you don't really want to. When you use the word "should" toward yourself, the emotional consequence is *guilt*. You feel guilty for not doing what you "should" have done.

Like this:

Thought: "At my age, I should be better at money."
Feeling: Guilt for being lazy/reckless/stupid/irresponsible, etc.

Thought: "I should be making a six-figure salary by now."
Feeling: Guilt for not being good enough at your job or not having the guts to ask for a raise.

Anytime you apply the word "should" to yourself, you're going to feel bad. When you direct "should" statements toward your money or other people, you feel anger, frustration, and resentment.

Like this:

Thought: "My client should have paid me by now, and she hasn't."

Feeling: Frustrated that she didn't keep her commitment and resentful that you're still delivering a service that she hasn't yet paid for.

Thought: "I've made decent money for ten years. My student loans should be paid off by now."
Feeling: Frustrated that your money isn't wiping out that debt and angry that you still have years left to make that monthly payment.

"Should" statements are automatic, irrational thoughts and they make you feel terrible about yourself, others, and your money. Any time you're setting an expectation for yourself, your money, or your partner, you're probably using a "should statement." This is why we need to transform expectations into agreements by changing "should" into "it would be nice" or "I wish." We need to change demands into requests.

MONEY TRUTH: Our dreams are bigger than our wallets.

It's easy to dream and expect more and more from your money. It's easy to expect more and more from yourself, your partner, and your life. What's not so easy is being patient, consistent, calm, steadfast, and flexible. If you're always rushing, pushing, forcing, plotting, racing, and expecting more and more, you're going to exhaust yourself, and burn out your relationships. Then everyone (yourself included) is going to want a long-ass break from you to recover.

You probably don't want your money to be like, "Yeah, so, let's take a break. Not like a break-up, but a really long period of time in which we don't see each other, speak to each other, or do anything together. In fact, just forget about me. Don't call me. I'll call you." How can you keep your money happy so that it wants to keep hanging out all the time and doing fun things with you? How can you prevent wanting to punch yourself in the face as you hustle to make more money? Three things:

1. Stop using "should statements"!
2. Set reasonable expectations (i.e. agreements).
3. Slow the fuck down.

I'll explain. They say the first step to recovery is admitting you have a problem. I have a problem. I'm probably one of the most impatient people you'll ever meet. But I'm in recovery, and I work on being more patient every single day. I'm a dreamer with huge goals, and I'm on a mission to make a massive impact and change the world for the better. Because I think, feel, and live big and boldly, my mind is constantly filled to the brim with new ideas, action steps, projects, plans, books, strategies, and goals. I want to do it all, have it all, and be it all **right now**.

I'm constantly telling myself that life is short; time is limited; and if I don't get it all done today, there won't be time left to fit it all in. This is such horse shit, but it sounds true in my mind and makes me feel anxious and panicked. I'm also constantly telling myself things like, "I should be making more money in my business. I should have published two books by now. I should work faster. I should spend more time connecting and building my platform instead of wasting time binge-watching *Virgin River*."

The "should statements" take over, and I feel the need to run. Like a sprinter trying to fly past all the other runners to cross the finish line first, I show up in my life with a fire under my butt, racing to get it all done. I put enormous pressure on myself to do all the work before I play and force myself to push past my limits so I can accomplish more and more and do everything perfectly the first time.

Once I reach a goal, I just set another one, and the race begins again. Before I know it, I'm exhausted, grumpy, and can't remember what my kids look like because I've had my face glued to my computer too long. I spend so much time telling myself I should be doing more, working faster and harder, that I lose sight of the process and the joy that comes from a slow and steady pace.

Sometimes, I treat my money the same way. I expect my online Money Therapy^R program to deliver thousands of dollars in the first few days of open enrollment, and if the results fall short of my expectations, I slap a crap ton of guilt on myself for not doing a better job. I expect my money to pay for my Audi, my editor, and the attorney who's working on my trademark registration. When there's not enough left over from all of that to get a massage and go out to dinner with my husband, I scold my money for not doing everything it should be doing.

I can get caught up in a toddler mentality, stomp my feet, and yell, "I want it! It's mine!" I'm not proud of it, but my awareness of this problem is growing and so are the action steps I'm taking to change my ways.

Every once in a while, my inner critic chimes in and tells me I should work longer and harder to make more money and have more stuff. I'm learning how to convince that part of my mind that less is more and it's not really about how much money I make. It's about **how much money I keep.** If you're nodding your head after reading my story and thinking I just described you, I think you'll find this next part particularly helpful.

MONEY TRUTH: You can have anything—just not everything. You can do anything—just not everything. You can be anything—just not everything.

Anything you want to have, do, or be takes time and patience. Knowing this truth will help you to set more reasonable expectations. It will help you to look at what you're willing and able to do in order to have, do, or be what you want. In essence, forming an agreement with yourself to go for those things or not.

It will help you to be fairer to your money and recognize that it can do a whole lot for you—just not everything at once. That will help you to choose what you really, really want now and what you're willing to wait for (knowing great things often take lots of time). Adjusting your financial expectations doesn't mean you're settling for less. It means you're making agreements with yourself that feel good and are setting goals that are actually achievable.

Chapter 33

Bringing Sexy Back

A fun and interesting sex life is a must-have in any great relationship—the money relationship included! Having a bland sex life, a non-existent sex life, or feeling pressure to have sex when you don't feel like it are common sticking points for many couples. But it doesn't have to be an issue in your money relationship as long as you know how to work around it.

Scrimping and saving all the time can be a real buzz kill. Never spending any money takes all the desire, joy, and fun out of life. If you deprive yourself of all your guilty pleasures, you're going to feel grumpy and miserable. That's no way to live. Besides, if you put yourself on a money diet, forbidding yourself from spending a dime, you'll eventually fall off the wagon and binge on a delicious spending spree. The key is to reduce expenses and needless spending while also giving yourself permission to indulge every once in a while.

When it comes to enjoying life's pleasures (like sex, vanilla lattes, massages, satin sheets, etc.) and enjoying what your money can do for you and the people you care about, it's all about *balance*. Too much of a good thing becomes a bad thing. Two Double Stuf Oreos? Delicious. Twenty Double Stuf Oreos? Gut-wrenching. A hot make-out sesh with a stranger? Sexy. A hot make-out sesh with *ten* strangers? Herpes. A mani & pedi twice a year? Heavenly. A mani & pedi twice a week? Financial killer.

Of course, you want to enjoy life and use your money to experience pleasure. That's what money is for. It might surprise you to know that human beings are inherently self-centered. It's in our genes to always be on the lookout for our best interests, and that's ensured our survival as a species. However, this feature can interfere with maintaining healthy relationships.

You're pursuing a relationship with your money because you know it will benefit you in many ways and thinking about all those benefits gets you all hot. But you have to cool your panties down before you go splurging because you also want to do what's best for the relationship, which includes staying on track with your financial goals and not spending beyond your means.

MONEY TRUTH: The key to becoming rich is to live far below your means while still living well.

As I mentioned before, I dramatically reduced my expenses when I got serious about paying off all my debt. I cut out everything I possibly could to free up money. Everything. I created monthly challenges for myself to see how little money I could spend. I competed against myself from one month to the next trying to outdo myself by spending less than the month before.

At first, it was really fun. I felt empowered, like I was finally taking control. But after a few months, it sucked balls. The initial high of freeing up money to put toward debt wore off fast, and all I wanted was to go shopping. Like an alcoholic who does so well abstaining from alcohol for so long and then relapses, I was like a shopaholic who was doing so well abstaining from retail therapy for so long and then binged at Banana Republic.

I needed my fix of pleasure. Why was I working so hard for my money if I couldn't ever enjoy it? What was even the point of having money if I couldn't use it to experience some freakin' pleasure? I'd gone for months without buying anything for myself and could feel my desire for pleasure build. It had been so long since I'd run my fingers down the smooth leather of a new pair of boots. I missed the smell of the Yankee candles that used to fill my house with hints of pumpkin and apple spice. I craved the feeling of hot stones on my back, body oil swirling around the base of my neck, and the divine pressure of a deep tissue massage. I wanted my daily vanilla lattes, damn it.

I was about to say, "Eff it!" to my debt payoff plan. It wasn't worth it. I couldn't live like that. I needed the treats. The rewards. I needed pleasure to be part of my relationship with money, or I was done.

During a money date, I laid it all out there for my money. My money was so understanding. It bought me a latte and an orange scone, and it agreed that for our relationship to be healthy and happy, it had to be filled with pleasure, but not wild, reckless, haphazard pleasure. Not impulsive, binge-shopping, constant-attention-seeking pleasure.

For the money relationship to be healthy, it has to be balanced. A little bit of modesty. A little bit of sex appeal.

A little bit of hard work. A little bit of reward. A little bit of self-discipline. A little bit of guilty pleasure.

You can have your cake and eat it too. A slice, not the whole damn thing! You can have your money going toward paying off all your debt, saving for retirement, and treating yourself to a nice dinner. You just can't have your money working its tail off for you, crushing all your financial goals, and treat you to surf n' turf, *and* a weekend at the spa, *and* buy you a new car, *and* renovate the bathroom.

It's just like sex. If you try to have sex three times a day, every day, your partner will probably start complaining, even if they love sex, because it's excessive. It's just too much. It takes away the novelty and distracts from the pleasure. But if you never try to have sex, like ever, your partner will probably start complaining because they love sex. And they want it with you because it feels good and they want to share that magic with you.

Your money doesn't like all-or-nothing either. It doesn't like blowing money on stuff several times a day, every day, and it's going to get grumpy if you try to do that. It doesn't like never spending money, like ever, and it's going to get annoyed if you act like a stingy Scrooge. There's no room in your money relationship for being a nymphomaniac or being a prude. If black is one extreme and white is the other, you want to live in the gray zone—the place in the middle where you and your money can work together and play together. The place where there's a balance between spending and saving, between paying off debt and rewarding yourself with treats.

Money Therapy Assignment

Guilty Pleasure Plan- create a plan for how you'll experience your favorite guilty pleasures while sticking to your financial goals

Schedule a date with your money and make a list of all the pleasures you want to enjoy as you work on improving your money relationship and begin managing your money better.

Then, pick out your favorites and link them each to a specific money goal. Once you reach that goal, celebrate with that pleasure and savor every minute of it like a hot make-out sesh!

Examples:

Money Goal: Payoff Auto Loan
Pleasure Plan: Celebrate with J. Lohr Chardonnay ($20) and sushi ($30)

Money Goal: Gain two new clients this month
Pleasure Plan: Celebrate with a whole day of reading books in pj's

Money Goal: Payoff ALL debt

Pleasure Plan: Celebrate with a beach vacation (use one month's worth of money that was going toward debt)

PART IX: MONEY MANAGEMENT-TAG TEAM IT WITH YOUR MONEY

Chapter 34

Money Management Basics

Striking a balance between spending and saving is something you'll be working on forever. Living in the gray zone and staying away from financial extremes is the key to a happy money relationship and financial prosperity. But how do you know if you're being faithful to your money and your budget? How do you figure out how much money to put toward debt and how much to save for retirement? You gotta work with your money like a team, so you're not going in one direction while your money is headed in another. This is what money management is all about.

Whenever I say the words "money management," I'm often greeted with grumbles, pouty faces, and deer-in-the-headlights expressions. I hear things like, "I'm just not good with numbers," or "I didn't major in finance so I'm never going to understand it." You too might have a false belief that you have to be good at math to manage your money well or that men are good with money and women just don't know what they're doing. In fact, a staggering fifty-one percent of women turn over financial management and decision-making to male partners because they lack confidence in their ability to manage money well. That statistic keeps me awake at night, and I'm on a mission to empower women to take a more active role in their financial lives so that statistic can change.

MONEY TRUTH: Managing money effectively has nothing to do with math or being good with numbers and everything to do with self-discipline.

You might be thinking, *Oh great! I have zero self-discipline. My spending is all over the place, and I don't even know where my money is going. How am I ever going to manage my money like a boss?* Time out. Nibble on some dark chocolate and relax. I got you, boo. We're in this together, and I'm here to help you develop some self-discipline hacks and get your money matters in check. But first, you need to know why self-discipline is necessary for financial success.

1. Self-discipline helps you to get organized and stay organized.

If you don't make it a point to sit down and review your finances, sort bills, write out what's due and when, and create systems for your money, you won't have a clue what's going on. I know it can be overwhelming to look at your financial situation, especially when you're in a financial crisis. It seems easier to just ignore it and hope it all goes away, but ignoring it got you in this position to begin with. Yes, it might be unpleasant to face the reality of your current financial picture, but by doing so and organizing that information in a logical way, you'll be able to discover what needs to happen to turn this "money mother" around.

2. Self-discipline helps you to create a plan.

You'll actually need to take the time, even if you don't like it, to create a plan for your money. If you don't have a plan for what you'll do with your money, you'll be all willy-nilly with it. Having a plan will also help you make informed and confident decisions about your money. (You won't need your husband, dad, or bro financial advisor to make financial decisions for you anymore!)

3. Self-discipline helps you stick to the plan.

The most important step here is sticking to the plan you make for your money, and that's where self-discipline comes in the most. You'll be tempted to veer off course and spend money on things you don't really need. There will always be people trying to sell you something, encouraging you to part with your hard-earned cash. Your brain is wired to always seek pleasure and avoid pain, so you'll often feel a pull to have what you want RIGHT NOW instead of waiting for it. You'll need self-discipline to avoid immediate gratification and stay on track with your financial goals (so they become a reality).

4. Self-discipline will help you to review your money plans regularly and see if it's still what you want.

Your money plan will serve as a living, breathing roadmap, which will need to be revised over time as your life and financial situation changes. You'll be crushing financial goals in no time, and then you'll need to create even bigger dreams for you and your money.

As you can see, self-discipline is far more important than addition and subtraction. The good news is that you can learn to be self-disciplined through practice. And the strategies and tools I'm about to give you will make money management feel fun and flirty.

Chapter 35

Every Dollar Needs a Job

Wanting money just for the sake of having it is pointless. Money needs a purpose. You need to create a "spending plan" that maps out all the jobs your money needs to be working on and when those jobs have to be done. And the plan must be realistic and achievable to avoid "money burnout."

So what exactly is a spending plan? It's a budget, but I hate that word. "Budget" makes me think of restriction and deprivation, like I can't spend money on anything. I steer clear of that word because it gives me a sense of dread.

"Spending plan" feels so much better to me. It gives me a sense of control (because that's what having a plan does), and it shows me where to go and how to get there. Call it whatever you want. The point is: you need one.

Your spending plan is basically your money's honey-do list. It breaks down jobs into categories and assigns an amount to each, so your money knows where it needs to go and what it needs to do.

Like this:

Rent: $500/month—due the 1st
Groceries: $400/month—$100 every week
Gas: $100/month—$50 every other week
Utilities: $150/month—due the 15th

If you don't give your money a specific job and tell it what to do, it's going to spend the afternoon on a shopping spree at Marshalls, getting a super expensive manicure, or impulsively splurging on all the crap advertised on Instagram. Give every single dollar a job. One dollar is just as important as five hundred dollars. Don't neglect the little guy. (I mean, little money.) Never underestimate the power of small amounts of money added up over time. A little here and a little there makes people millionaires.

Chapter 36

Buckets of Cash

Before I found myself in Money Therapy[R], I made a big money mistake. I didn't use a spending plan. I didn't even know what it was, and I didn't know where my money was going. Hell, I didn't even know how much money was coming into my business or how much money was going out. All I knew was that I didn't have enough money, the bills always seemed to outweigh the revenue, and I found myself basically working for free because there was nothing left to pay myself after paying all the monthly bills.

I was pretty clueless when it came to money. I just kept working, paying the bills (sometimes late), and hoping for the best. My money didn't have a job, and I didn't know how to set up money buckets to help me know how much money I needed for everything I spent money on. There was very little thought given to what I wanted my money to do for me. It was a *terrible* system because it wasn't a system at all. It was a fly-by-the-seat-of-my-pants method to managing my money, and it led to $87,000 of debt, my business being in the red for more months than I like to admit, and suffering from major money drama and financial stress.

One of the worst feelings in the world is working your tail off for nothing. Zero dollars. I was too scared to sit down and look at my money or figure out how much my business was making and where it was all going. I was afraid of what I'd find; I was afraid it would prove that I was terrible with money and destined for bankruptcy.

So, I did what any girl would do when faced with an uncomfortable situation: I avoided it. I hid from it. Seriously, when the bills came in the mail, I would stuff the unopened envelopes in the back of my desk drawer and try to forget about them. Then more envelopes would be delivered, this time with red stamps on the front that read: "Second Notice." I would stuff, stuff, stuff them...way back there.

Avoiding, hiding, and stuffing only made my problems worse, and not just financially. I lost sleep at night worrying about those bills hidden in my desk drawer and started having stomach aches and chest pain from the anxiety of it all. I became chronically irritable and snappy, even at my furry pal, Clover (who's the sweetest creature in the whole wide world).

Then, I started getting sick—a lot. Constant colds and headaches. The money stress was really taking a toll on me and my whole life! I hit rock bottom when I realized that if I didn't get my money matters in order, we'd lose our house. The pain I felt at the thought of making my little family homeless motivated me to do what needed to be done.

I sat down with a gallon of coffee and gave some serious thought to what I needed money for and how I wanted to use it to make my business (and life) better. I set aside a whole afternoon for my money, opened up my bank account, pulled out old bills, and started investigating. I began to examine what I'd been using money for up to that point. What was actually happening? What was going well? How much money did I have? Where had all the money gone? During that first-ever money date, I finally got honest with myself about what wasn't working, what I needed to stop doing with my money, and what I needed to start doing with it instead.

Much to my surprise, I realized that I was throwing money at things I didn't really value, like advertising that didn't boost business, the latest shiny gadgets that did nothing but keep me distracted and comparing myself to others, and clothes and shoes that ended up forgotten in the back of my closet. And because I was spending my money all willy-nilly, I didn't have money for the things I really wanted, like the cross-country road trip that would give me a sense of freedom and adventure or the writing class that would help me express my creativity but wasn't "within my price range." My life wasn't what I wanted it to be because I wasn't in control of my money.

So, I created **buckets of cash** based on my deepest values, the things that are most important in life. A bucket for **freedom**. A bucket for **creativity**. A bucket for **growth**. A bucket for spirituality. A bucket for **health**. Then, every month, I added a certain amount of money to each bucket. That meant eliminating random shopping trips and items from Facebook ads from my money's to-do list and replacing them with jobs that added more meaning and joy to my life.

For me, the buckets symbolized the categories in my spending plan (a.k.a. budget). For you, the buckets might symbolize items on a spreadsheet, envelopes that you actually put cash in and pull from when you need it, or a designated savings account at your bank. Literally drawing my buckets of cash on paper, being intentional about how much money I spent and what I spent it on, and checking in on my money to make sure it was doing its job was life-changing. I finally had money for the things I wanted. My business started to become more profitable. I had control over my finances and knew exactly what my money was up to and how much was available to me. I'll bet you a bucket of cash that you'll experience the very same thing when you create your buckets and give your money a job.

Chapter 37

Own It

In therapy, we talk a lot about ownership and taking responsibility for the ways we create problems in our own lives. Honestly, it's hard AF to own your crap and admit to mistakes, bad decisions, and unhealthy behaviors. It's even harder to not judge yourself for it.

But the therapist's office is a judgment-free zone because judging yourself for what's happened in the past is completely unhelpful and does nothing but put you in a salty mood. Yes, you need to get honest with yourself about what isn't working when it comes to the ways you manage your money (or don't manage it). You'll need to take responsibility for getting to where you are now and own it. But there's a way to go about it that will make you feel less like a hot mess.

Focus on your strengths. It might not seem like it, but you're actually doing some really great things with your money; you just aren't aware of it yet. Start by looking for what's going well. You paid a bill on time? Great job! You can do it again! You paid more than the minimum payment on your credit card? Fantastic! You made an extra sale last month and pocketed an extra $150? You're amazing!

MONEY TRUTH: You can't build on broken. You have to build on strengths.

The strengths you find in yourself and your situation serve as the foundation to build your money relationship upon. You can replicate what's already working, do more of it, or tweak it slightly so it works even better for you. Rather than starting with failures, mistakes, and all the bad decisions you've made, start with your strengths and find what's working. That way, you'll know what to keep doing moving forward.

Be a private investigator and spy on your money. Pretend that you've been hired as a private investigator to spy on your money. It's not personal; it's business. It's not about how you feel about your money. It's a neutral, objective investigation to find answers to questions. You have a job to do: find out where your money is going and what it's doing. Take note of all the dirty deeds it's been up to over the past few years. Take screenshots. Track it. Follow it. Don't let your money out of your sight for a minute until you put all the pieces of the puzzle together.

Just look at the facts. Don't get all emotional or critical of yourself. Don't be a Judgy-McJudgerson. Just see what the heck is going on with your money so you can then figure out what to STOP doing, what to CONTINUE doing, and what to START doing.

Chapter 38

Money Management Magic

Once you have a good idea of what's going on with your money, you'll need some tools to help you manage it well. Why are money management tools important? Well, it's like trying to bake a cake without a cake pan. It's damn near impossible. Baking calls for pans, an electric mixer, and measuring cups to make the job faster, easier, and successful. Same goes for managing your money.

You could do it the old-fashioned way by keeping cash in a sock drawer and pulling it out when you need to replace the laundry detergent, just like you could stir the cake batter by hand and weigh all the ingredients instead of measuring them. But that would take forever. Let's do it the easy, fast, and fun way and put some tools in your hands.

The money management tools you absolutely need include a spending plan tool and debt payoff tool. You could create a spending plan with pen and paper. You can begin by writing down each category and jotting down how much money to put toward each, but you'll spend an enormous amount of time going back to that paper to write down every transaction and run the numbers. Don't be so hard on yourself. Invest in budgeting software that does the heavy lifting for you.

My favorite spending plan software is You Need a Budget (YNAB). It's inexpensive, and you get your first month free to try it out. I love YNAB because it provides you with an instant template so you can just fill in your specific info. It gives you a list of common, monthly expenses to choose from or you can add your own. The entire system keeps everything organized so you don't have to do it yourself.

The system also makes it easy to import transactions from your bank account, so you don't have to manually enter each purchase you make. The program shows you how much money is available in each category to spend and alerts you if you've overspent. You can also generate easy-to-read reports to see your entire financial picture at a glance and track spending and saving over time. A tool like YNAB helps keep you accountable, self-disciplined, and organized. Your money will crush so hard on you if you get YNAB!

When it comes to creating a debt payoff plan, it might seem impossible to pay off all your debt and live debt-free, but I know you can do it. Living debt-free is truly the only way to experience real financial freedom because if you carry debt, you don't own what you have; you're just borrowing what you have. That's not freedom, friend.

Imagine having the money to pay all the bills as soon as they arrive, thousands of dollars in a savings account for emergencies, a fully-funded retirement account, and the means to pay for your kids (or someone else's) to go to college. This is what's possible when you don't have debt.

When you don't have monthly debt payments, you free up hundreds or thousands of dollars in your spending plan to put toward these long-term financial goals. Then, you get to sit back and watch your money grow.

It will take some time, but with self-discipline, consistency, and persistence, you can wipe out all your debt and live debt-free for good. The first step in creating a debt payoff plan is to take an inventory of all your debts:

- Mortgages
- Business Loans
- Personal Loans
- Home Equity Line of Credit (HELOC)
- Student Loans
- Auto Loans
- Credit Cards

It's probably not going to feel great when you do this. If you feel anything like I felt when I did a debt inventory, you'll feel panicked and overwhelmed, like a ball and chain are weighing you down. You might feel afraid and hopeless about ever breaking free from the burden of all that debt. But don't fret, my pet. It's not hopeless. You can do this. Now, it won't be easy. You'll have to make some (temporary) sacrifices, which will be hard but worth it. Pinky promise.

See, something magical happens when you finally take control of your finances, spend intentionally, and pay off all your debt. Your money starts swooning over you and wants to love up on you all the time. Before you know it, your money will be asking you what else it can do for you—

how it can make your life better, easier, and more pleasurable. You'll be able to save money like never before and afford anything you want. But first, you need to pay off all your debt and gain full control over your spending. Here's what you need to do:

- Know what's happening with your money (by creating and sticking to your spending plan)
- Reduce expenses to free up money in your spending plan (and put the extra toward debt)
- Increase your income (so you can put even more money toward debt and wipe it out fast)

You already know what you need to do to get a good feel for what's happening with your money, and once you identify your latte factors (inexpensive items you buy frequently), you'll be able to start reducing needless expenses. Little amounts of money spent often add up to a lot of dough. As you stop spending money on those latte factors, you can start taking that money and putting it toward your debt, but you'll want to start eliminating even more expenses than just those.

If you wanna get serious about crushing debt, you gotta seriously cut out spending on as many things as possible. I cut out haircuts and colors, manicures, cable TV, eating out more than once a week, brand name everything, and retail-priced anything. I didn't go on vacation for two years, didn't have fancy date nights, and didn't spend a ton of money on Christmas gifts.

If you're cringing right now and thinking, *OMG, I can NOT give up my manicures or HGTV! You're crazy talking right now!* I feel you. It's a little ouchy at first, but it gets better. Giving up those little indulgences for just a little while, like a year or two, will give you a sense of power, freedom, control, and peace of mind. Besides, you might not miss those things as much as you think you will.

Increasing your income can help you pay off your debt at lightning speed, too. There are a million different ways to make money, and when you're working on paying off debt, nothing should be beneath you. Hustle for a little bit for your money so you can relax and enjoy luxuries after your debt has disappeared.

Clean out your closet and sell the stuff you no longer want or need. Put the money toward your debt. Ask your boss for a raise. Bartend or wait tables part-time to make some extra moolah. Drive an Uber. Sell arts and crafts on Etsy. Sell your fancy car, pay off the loan, and buy a cheap beater to get around. Start charging for the skills you've been giving away for free, like proofreading content, helping write resumes, or giving advice on how to create Instagram Stories. You've got mad skills that other people need and will be happy to pay for. Ask and you shall receive! Remember, **every dollar counts**! Make that money and give it the job of paying off your debt!

Chapter 39

Automatic Lover

What do you think is the single most important thing when it comes to creating financial freedom? Money dates? They're important, but that's not it. Making a crap ton of money? That helps, but it's not absolutely necessary. Penny-pinching, scrimping, and saving every dollar? Stop it. A life without guilty pleasures isn't worth living. The answer is compounding interest.

Say what? Oh love, compounding interest is like your money's best friend—one who's super cool and a blast to hang out with. Compounding interest will be like the best man at your wedding, "the guy" you're always happy to see, the person your kids call their "favorite uncle" even though you're not blood-related. But here's the deal with compounding interest: It's awesome and all, but it's not going to be the one to make the first move and reach out to you. You gotta reach out to it, invite it to hang out with you, and give it a good reason to be part of your life. **You make the first move and invite compounding interest to bless your life with its presence by automatically, systematically,** and consistently depositing money into your investment accounts every month.

Cuteness and analogies aside, here's what compounding interest really is and how it works. Compound interest is the addition of interest to the amount you deposit. In other words, its interest on top of interest. When you deposit money into your investment account, it accrues interest. If you leave it there and don't withdrawal the money or the interest that you earn on it, you're essentially reinvesting the interest it accrued while it sat there. So, the money keeps growing and growing, and then you earn even more interest on top of that! Here's an example:

Let's say you deposit $100 into an investment account that pays 5% annually. At the end of the year, you would gain $5 in interest. But in the next year, you'll be blessed by a visit from good, old compounding interest (and it will actually stick around forever until you withdraw all your money). You'll earn interest on your initial deposit, and you'll earn interest on the interest you just earned.

Then, the interest you earn the second year will be more than the year before because your account balance is now $105, not $100. Even though you didn't make any deposits, your earnings will accelerate, like this:

Year One: An initial deposit of $100 earns 5% interest, or $5, bringing your balance to $105.

Year Two: Your $105 earns 5% interest, or $5.25; your balance is now $110.25.

Year Three: Your balance of $110.25 earns 5% interest, or $5.51; your balance is now $115.76.

The more you deposit, the more interest you earn, the bigger the snowball, and the more money you have in the end. If you invested $100 **every month** at a 5% return, you'd make $110 in interest for the year. That's $110 of **free money!** Money that you didn't have to trade your time for!

Compounding interest is basically how your money makes money. It's like helping your money get ready for work in the morning (depositing into your investment account), sending your money out the door (putting your money toward different stocks/bonds), and then enjoying the paycheck your money brings home every month (collecting interest from those stocks/bonds). Every day, every week, and every month your money goes to work and makes you more money, and the more you help it get ready to go to work every day (by not overspending and depositing as much as possible every month), the more money it will earn.

When your money is making enough money to pay your living expenses, you don't have to work anymore. You can chillax by the pool with a Mai Tai and your favorite glossy magazine. But before you get carried away in a fantasy of never working again and getting baked in the sun, you gotta get in the habit of helping your money get ready for work every day (a.k.a. making consistent deposits into your investment account). It needs to be part of your everyday routine. It needs to be so automatic that you don't have to think about it. If you have to think about it, make a decision about it, or take some sort of action step, it won't happen.

Budgeting basically saved my money relationship, helped me get clear on where my money was going, and kept me from overspending. But there was one big mistake I was still making: I wasn't saving money in my investments. It wasn't even really on my radar. I thought I was doing a great job being in control of my money, especially my spending, because I was giving every dollar a job in my spending plan. But I wasn't giving my money the job of making more money. I was clueless. I was still spending more than I should have been. The money I was spending on little extras should have been going into investment accounts so I didn't have to work until I die.

Why was I increasing the amount spent on guilty pleasures instead of increasing my retirement savings? I was experiencing a psychological phenomenon called "hedonic adaptation," which is the tendency we all have to adapt quickly to changes in our lives and return to a baseline level of happiness. Once my business started making money, I quickly adapted to that change and made decisions with my money so I could experience the same level of happiness I did before my financial crisis began.

Before I was in the red, I wouldn't hesitate to spend money on little luxuries and conveniences. Daily lattes. Trendy clothes. Monthly massages. When I had zero cash, all of that went out the window, but the minute money was flowing back in, hedonic adaptation took over and motivated me to start spending money again on things I liked but didn't really need. I was prioritizing temporary happiness (retail therapy) over long-term financial growth (investing).

Once I realized what I was doing and became more aware of the power of compounding interest that I was missing out on, I quickly made changes in my approach to my spending plan. I basically flipped the process around. I started paying the bills that absolutely needed to be paid first (to keep my business running). Next, I took 15% of whatever was left over and deposited it into my investment account. I then paid myself a salary based on what remained. If there was any money left over after that, I spent it on the little luxuries I wanted.

This method worked out really well...at first. It controlled my spending so I wasn't constantly increasing my standard of living as my income increased, and it allowed me to finally contribute to my investments like a boss. That was until I got too busy and forgot to make the deposits altogether. When things really took off in my practice, I was seeing almost twenty clients a week, hiring and training new staff, credentialing with additional insurance companies, doing all the marketing, writing blogs, and still taking care of my family. Making the transfer from my business checking to my investment account was near the bottom of my priority list. Were all the bills paid? Yes. Ok, that's good enough.

Then after a few months, I'd see a really hefty amount in my account and wonder why there was so much money there, only to realize my cash had been sitting there waiting to be transferred and not making a dime of interest in the meantime. "Doh!" Oddly enough, logging into my account and transferring money just seemed like too much of a hassle. It was an obstacle to investing that was derailing my financial progress and costing me money. But there was a way to blast through that barrier: AUTOMATION.

Automatic transfer from one account to another is the most genius invention ever! I started using it. And it worked! Because of automation, I never forgot to pay myself first or contribute to my investment account again because I never had to remember to begin with! (This is one of the only aspects of the money relationship that you really can set it and forget it!) My money became my automatic lover.

Chapter 40

Eliminate the Decision

You already know that consumerism and retail therapy won't really make you happier (at least not in the long term), but the financial security and freedom you get from having a big, fat investment account that pays you to do nothing will make you happier. The cure for hedonic adaptation is to pay yourself first. Put a chunk of money in your investment account and only spend what's left over.

Learn from my mistakes and keep in mind that you won't contribute to your investment accounts regularly if you have to think about it. If you have to decide to save and invest instead of spend every month, you'll likely make the wrong choice. Remember, your brain is always seeking pleasure and trying to avoid pain. Spending money is often pleasurable. Logging into your checking account and watching the balance go down as you transfer funds to your investment account brings about a certain degree of pain.

If you see there's money available, you'll immediately start dreaming of all the things you could do with it. A full day at the spa sounds so good right now. Your laptop is super old and could crash any minute. A new one is a necessity, right? Who has time for cleaning toilets? That extra money could pay for a housekeeper! You'll tell yourself that you deserve all these things because you've worked so hard and should experience some damn pleasure already!

I agree. You do deserve to experience pleasure and rewards for your hard work. But think back to your values for a minute. Do those shiny objects align with your values and what's most important to you in life? Do those things give you the financial freedom and security you (also) deserve? Do those things *really* make you happier in the long run? What would make you the happiest? To have those things now but work yourself to the bone? Or not have those things right now and have absolute freedom to work or play as you choose?

When it comes right down to it, you're essentially choosing between time and money. **Money is basically a repository of the time we put into earning it.** You can always make more money, but time is of finite supply. Every dollar you save instead of spending is giving you more time to do what you want. Instead of using your money to reward yourself for your work, use it as a tool to buy back your time.

Money Therapy Assignment

Give Every Dollar a Job

Poof! Out of nowhere, $250 just landed in your lap! WOOT WOOT!

Now, you need to decide what to do with it. You need to give your money a job. Will you save it? Put it toward paying off debt? Indulge in a full day at the spa? Give that $250 a job (or multiple jobs); jobs that make you want to snuggle up to your money and whisper words of appreciation for everything it's doing for you.

Draw a bucket for each thing you intend to spend money on. Label each bucket with the job you want your money to do and list the amount you'll need for that job under each one. Feel free to color the buckets, add designs and stickers, or draw little hearts. Have fun and make it your own!

All done? Perfection! Here's what to do next:

- Add this job to your budget/spending plan and list the $250 in that category so it's there and ready to be used when you need it.

- Or use that money today by depositing it into an account, writing a check for a bill, or buying something wonderful with it.
- Write a little thank-you note to your money for showing up and making your life better and brighter.
- Shout it from the rooftops that your money is awesome and you're putting it to good use! Tell your BFF, your partner, or post it on social media. Talking about the cool things you're doing with your money inspires others to give their money a job too.

PART X: PROTECTING YOUR MONEY MARRIAGE

Chapter 41

Prenuptial Agreement

As you near the end of this book, I hope you can look back at your money relationship and see how far you've come. The "on-again, off-again" relationship you used to have with your money has been repaired. Now you're head-over-heels for your finances and ready to put a ring on it.

You and your money have taken your relationship to the next level, and all you can think about is heading to the altar. You're mentally writing out your money marriage vows and planning your honeymoon to Fiji. But before you get to all the fun stuff, you've got to deal with some of the more serious stuff that comes along with this type of commitment.

Your money has asked you for a **prenuptial agreement**. Hearing that might make you be all like, "WTF? Why would my money want a prenup? Does my money think this relationship is destined to end in disaster? Is my money uncertain about our relationship? Does my money think I'm going to betray it? AHHHHH!" Deep breath, love.

Prenups aren't so scary when you know what they really are, and having a prenuptial agreement with your money is actually really smart. It doesn't mean your money doesn't love you, nor does your money think you'll "divorce." It means your money wants to protect you from financial pain in the future and make sure you've got everything you need to live a great life with as little financial stress as possible. Aww, isn't your money sweet?

So, what is a prenup? A prenuptial agreement is a written document that outlines what each person has acquired prior to the marriage (what each person is bringing with them) and what each person is entitled to if the marriage dissolves (what each person leaves with). The agreement protects your rights and your assets (all your money, property, and possessions) and protects you from taking on your partner's liabilities (all of their outstanding debts).

How does this apply to your money relationship? Well, you want your money relationship to stay strong, and I'm sure you want to make more money over time. If you aren't clear on where you started and how much money (assets) you came into the "marriage" with and how much debt (liabilities) you started with, you won't be able to see your progress as you move forward in your money marriage and make big changes to your finances. Drafting a prenup for your money marriage is simply a fun way to outline your **net worth**, which is the difference between your **assets** (what you own) and your **liabilities** (what you owe).

Stay with me here. When people hear words like "assets" and "liabilities," their eyes start to glaze over, and I get lots of big, bored yawns. I often hear whining like, "This stuff is so boring and dull. Why do I have to do this? Can't my financial advisor just take care of this for me? Who cares about net worth?"

I'm with you. I can totally relate to feeling bored out of my mind when it comes to crunching numbers and calculating stuff like this, which is why I'm putting a fun twist on the whole thing, because this really is important. Not only is it incredibly useful for you to know where you began on your financial journey, but other people are gonna need this information, too. If you ever want to get a loan to buy a house, car, a business, or anything else, the bank is likely going to ask you for a list of your assets and liabilities because they need proof that you have the means to repay the loan! It's always better when you have it at the ready so you aren't scrambling at the last minute trying to figure it out.

"But wait! I plan on living debt-free like you told me I should. So why would I ever need a loan?" Great question! Ideally, you will live debt free forever, but sometimes a big opportunity comes along that you really, really want to take advantage of (because it will create even better financial growth), and it costs big money that you don't have on hand. A loan will make it possible for you to seize the opportunity and make more money in the end.

A mortgage loan is a great example of this. Remember the rental property in Colorado that I sold and then used the profit to buy my dream farmette? I took out a mortgage on a house when I bought it because I didn't have cash for it. I paid $165,000 for the house in 2009. I moved out of the house in 2011 and rented it out from 2011 to 2018. The rent I collected paid for the mortgage, and there was an extra $500/month that was profit for me. Then, I sold the house in 2018 for $325,000 and walked away with $160,000 profit. See what a good idea it was to take out a loan to buy that house all those years ago?! But before I could get approved for the loan, I had to provide the bank with a list of my assets and liabilities, and I had to do it fast before someone else came along and bought the house I wanted.

Ok, so let's start drafting your prenup. Just like a marital prenup outlines what each person brings to the marriage (both assets and liabilities), your money prenup maps out what assets and liabilities you have. Before we dive into the nitty-gritty of what you own and what you owe, I have to warn you: This might not feel great. When you start looking at real numbers and thinking about net worth, you're likely to think about self-worth, too. You might look at how the numbers stack up and realize you really don't own that much and your debt far outweighs what you have saved in cash. You might look at your current salary compared to your total liabilities and feel like it will never be enough to dig you out of that hole, which can make you feel like you're not good enough.

In other words, as you work through this session, you might feel worse before you start to feel better. Therapy is like that sometimes. When you dredge stuff up, it stings. When you look at what's been buried underneath, it's ugly. But once you sort through it, make sense of it, and reframe it a bit, it takes on new meaning and then you can feel better about the whole thing. Let me share my own experience of this, so you can see what I'm talking about.

Chapter 42

More than Dollars and Cents

Before I met my husband, I didn't give too much thought to how much money I made. I always felt that if I were making more money than my family did, I was doing well for myself. The most my grandfather ever made as a truck driver was $50,000 a year. So, when I got my first "big girl" job making $53,000 a year, I was thrilled.

Then Tom came into my life, and he **really** cared about how much money he made. He was on a mission to make as much money as he possibly could, which was why he studied medicine and became a physician assistant. He earned a six-figure salary from the day he started working and continues to.

My financial situation looked much different. When I left that first "big girl" job to move back home to Pennsylvania, I stopped working for other people and started my mental health practice. I thought I'd make more money working for myself in those first few years than I did working for a company, but that's not how it played out.

It took almost seven years for my practice to become profitable, and I spent hundreds of hours working for free to get my business off the ground. As I hustled in my practice every week, bringing home peanuts for a paycheck, I saw my husband actually putting in fewer hours than me and bringing home ten times more. That felt like shit.

I tried reminding myself that my values were different from Tom's, and while making as much money as possible was most important to him, doing something I love and being my own boss was most important to me. When I sat down to map out how much money I really had and how much money I still owed, I was ready to kick my dinky business to the curb in exchange for a big, fat corporate paycheck. And Tom encouraged me to trade in my entrepreneurial dreams for more dollars and cents!

I felt like a failure and figured Tom saw me that way too. I was putting tremendous pressure on myself and my business to hurry up and make some damn money already, but it wasn't happening as fast as I wanted it to. I felt like I was bringing our financial life down instead of building it up "like I was supposed to," and that also felt really crappy.

For some reason though, I felt deep down that my private practice was a gold mine, and if I just kept at it, one day I would strike it big and be set for life. I would often say this to Tom when he would start harassing me about how I "should be making at least $60,000 a year with a master's degree," but he didn't believe in me or my business like I did. And quite frankly, I didn't need him to.

I wasn't sure exactly how I was going to make my business super profitable or when it would finally yield the profits

I wanted. I just knew that I didn't want to give up, and I'd keep trying different things until I figured it out. **I kept reminding myself that my self-worth is NOT determined by my net worth.** In fact, it's the other way around. The value I place on myself determines how much money I make.

I had to remember that I'm so much more than dollars and cents, no matter what anyone else has to say about it. And while I wasn't bringing in the six-figure salary that Tom was, I was offering value in a number of other ways, like running our whole damn household, caring for our babies, cooking all our meals, keeping everyone in clean clothes, building a business one step at a time, and physically/emotionally supporting my husband so he could focus on his work and earn that big, fat paycheck for us.

Instead of feeling resentful toward my husband about him making more money than me, I replaced resentment with gratitude because his paycheck freed me up to work on my business and grow it slowly and organically instead of being forced to work a day job while building my business just to make ends meet.

When I sat down to run the numbers again (eight years later) and compared my net worth today to what it was back then, I realized that I was contributing to our financial life that whole time in ways I didn't even see. All the decisions I'd made about what property to buy and sell and when to do it were contributions to our financial life. All the decisions I'd made in my business to grow it over time were contributions to our financial life. All the decisions I'd made related to creating our spending plan, mapping out a debt payoff plan, and stashing money in an emergency fund were all contributing to our financial life. (BTW, my husband was great at making money but wasn't doing jack shit with managing it. I consider myself our financial hero.)

For the record, I was right about my private practice being a gold mine. "Striking gold" took SO much longer than I thought it would, but I'm proud to say that as of this very moment, I work about five hours a week in my private practice and earn about $80,000 a year. Now Tom's the one wondering why the hell he has to work three times as much to make the same amount!

I'm telling you all of this because I don't want you to feel bad about yourself when you look at your assets and liabilities. Those numbers aren't about YOU. They're just numbers, but those numbers help you to see where you are now and where you want to go, so you can take steps toward living your best financial life.

You gotta remember; it's not all about the money. Money is just the cherry on top of the sundae. It's not the sundae itself. YOU are the sundae: the big, delicious scoop of ice cream at the center of it all. You offer value to the world in so many different ways; that value doesn't come with a price tag. So, as you work on this assignment at the end of the chapter, don't get discouraged if your liabilities outweigh your assets. It's important to know your net worth, but you also need to know your self-worth. Those are two different things.

Be smart and get this down on paper. Draft your prenup for your money marriage in such a way that it's ready to hand over at a moment's notice if a big opportunity comes your way. Keep your prenup in a safe place so you can reference it in the future. Run the numbers again and see how far you've come.

Wherever you're at now is not where you'll stay. You're on a direct path to financial liberation, financial success, and ongoing financial growth. Writing out your assets and liabilities is simply one marker on the road to financial freedom.

Chapter 43

Home-wreckers

Let's shift gears now and talk about how to protect your money marriage after you walk down the aisle and say, "I do." Have you ever felt super protective of your partner? Like when someone comes along and has his/her/their eye on your hottie and starts being all flirtatious. You're watching this whole thing go down, wondering who the hell they think they are coming in and trying to steal your sweetie.

This only ever happened to me once in my twelve-year marriage, but when it did, it totally sucked. My husband met "Jackie" when she came to our house to buy an elliptical machine we were selling on Craigslist. Over the course of the entire transaction, she interacted with my husband a total of two or three times. Jackie was married, but oddly enough, her husband didn't come with her to load the elliptical. She had four guy friends help her load and unload the machine.

Long story short, Jackie felt like it was ok to have text conversations with my husband after that about really personal stuff, like how her husband wanted her to have kids, but she wasn't sure she wanted them. WTF? Why would you talk about that with a stranger? Especially someone else's husband? I felt super uncomfortable about the whole thing, but my husband reassured me I had nothing to worry about.

Fast forward *one year*. I found out that Jackie had been texting Tom every couple of months, and he kept responding to her! I had this gut feeling that this woman was after my man. She was being slow and sneaky about it too, which was smart on her part because my husband didn't pick up on the signs. He thought it was completely innocent.

I've invested a tremendous amount of time and energy into having a good marriage, and I wasn't about to let anyone jeopardize that. I had to guard my marriage. You have to guard your money marriage in the same way.

I'm not saying that someone is going to come along and try to steal all your money from your bank account (although that could happen) or that you need to call people up and firmly tell them to stay the hell away from your cash (like I respectfully told Jackie to stop texting my husband). But you've worked hard to make the financial progress you've made. You've invested so much into this money relationship, and you don't want your money to suddenly be taken away.

This chapter is all about the dangers that threaten your money. Let's call them "home-wreckers" for fun. I'll also show you how to protect your money marriage from them. You're making great progress and gaining so much momentum in gaining financial freedom. Now we need to safeguard your money, so it lasts a lifetime.

There are dangers out there that can threaten your money marriage, just like there are "home-wreckers" out there that can threaten your actual marriage (or any romantic relationship for that matter).

Here's a list of "home-wreckers":

- An accident or major illness when you are uninsured or underinsured with health insurance
- A fire, act of Mother Nature, or natural disaster that damages your home or other real estate properties without being properly insured
- A separation or divorce where assets are divided and you go from two incomes to one
- An unexpected expense or loss of income due to loss of a job, a lull in business, or the need to take an extended absence from income-producing work
- The death of a partner/spouse/parent, which results in loss of their wages, funeral expenses, and their liabilities being passed on to you
- Your own death, which compromises the money you've worked hard to provide for your family and eliminates your income for them

After looking at that list, you might be freaking out, breathing into a paper bag, and feeling frozen by all the terrible things that could ruin your money marriage and leave you broke. Don't sweat, my pet! There are ways to protect yourself from all of these dangers. You just need to put some protection plans into place, so you and your money can be together forever, no matter what storm blows through your life. And we know **there will be storms.** You can count on it. You can expect them. Bad shit is bound to happen.

Take the housing market crash of 2008 for example. A big storm blew through, and tons of people lost their houses. Take the global pandemic of 2020 as another example. Coronavirus arrived, and tons of people lost their incomes. No one saw those things coming, so it was impossible to prepare for those exact scenarios. But the people who had taken measures to protect their money from *anything* rolled out of that shit smelling like roses. You want to be in that camp too: prepared for anything. Calm, cool, and collected.

There are some super important protection plans you need to put in place to save your money marriage from any and all "home-wreckers":

<u>1. Emergency fund</u>

You need an emergency fund. There are two types or phases to emergency funds. The first type occurs at the beginning of your debt payoff journey. You'll want to stash just $1,000 in a high-yield savings account to have on hand for emergencies. That's all you need while you're working on paying off all your debt because you want every penny to go to debt, not sit in a traditional savings account doing nothing.

The second type occurs after you've paid off all your debt. You'll want to save three to six months of expenses in your emergency fund. Just look at your spending plan, and you'll know how much your living expenses are each month. Keep this larger emergency fund money in a high-yield savings account so it can earn interest (make more money) while it sits there. Only use this money if there is a legit emergency. (A sale at Macy's is not an emergency.)

<u>2. Living will</u>

No one likes to think about their own death, but you need to for the sake of your family. A living will is an important protection plan because it outlines your wishes related to end of life decisions, who will inherit your assets and liabilities, who will care for your children if you and your partner both die, and so much more. If people don't know what you want, they won't be able to make sure your estate is handled in the way you like or that your wishes are carried out.

A living will also reduces the likelihood that family members will argue and fight over what you would have wanted because it's all mapped out for them. So, when the shit hits the fan, your loved ones won't have to deal with a family feud in addition to grieving the loss of YOU. It's best to work with an attorney to draft a living will, and this is definitely something you and your partner will want to do together so you're both on the same page.

3. Life/Property insurance policies

Speaking of dying, do you have a life insurance policy that will pay out a death benefit to your beneficiary if you die? If not, you need one, especially if your beneficiary/partner is dependent on your income. Likewise, if you depend on your partner's income, they/he/she needs a life insurance policy that would pay you a death benefit in the event of their/his/her death. You really don't need life insurance policies on children. You don't get a financial benefit from your children because you don't rely on wages from them.

There are two types of life insurance:

Term Life Insurance: costs a minimal monthly fee and pays out a specific amount if you die. You determine the amount of coverage you want, and your monthly premium is based on that and your age. When you die, your beneficiary gets the money.

Whole Life Insurance: costs significantly more each month but works as an investment tool in addition to providing a death benefit. Once you've contributed a certain amount to the policy, you can take a loan against it. If you don't pay back the loan before you die, it's simply deducted from your death benefit, and the money you contribute each month increases in value over time.

A financial planner or advisor can help you decide which policy is right for you, but heed this warning: whole life insurance policies offer big commission checks to financial advisors. So, make sure you're working with someone who has your best interests in mind and isn't just in it for their own financial gain.

Property insurance/homeowner's insurance protects your home and all its contents. It also covers you if someone gets injured on your property and sues you. You need this coverage to protect you from acts of Mother Nature. Hurricanes. Tornados. Hailstorms. Fire. Floods.

4. Health insurance

Health insurance can keep you alive. You know the deal on health insurance, so I won't bore you. You need preventative health care and screenings and coverage for illnesses or injures. If you have a day job that offers you insurance, you can get it through your employer, or you might be able to get on your partner's insurance policy.

What if you're single or self-employed? Most people think they have to purchase health insurance through the

Marketplace, but they find it ridiculously expensive and can only get terrible policies that have huge annual deductibles.

You have two alternatives to the Marketplace:

1. Put aside money in your budget every month for medical expenses and pay cash for your care.

If you're young and healthy, this might be a good option, at least until you're making enough money to cover an insurance premium each month. My husband and I were uninsured for seven years and paid cash for our care, even the monthly medication my husband took for a pre-existing condition.

But there is some risk involved in not being insured. If you're involved in an accident or diagnosed with a serious illness, it could destroy your finances, which brings me to the second alternative.

2. Buy private insurance through a broker.

You know how insurance agents shop around for the best auto insurance policy for you? Well, there are insurance agents who also shop around for the best health insurance policy for you, too. A health insurance broker will look for the best plan to fit your health needs and your budget.

Tom and I now have private health insurance that covers our family of four for $328 a month. It's a limited policy that covers a certain dollar amount for each procedure/doctor visit, so we just make sure we work with providers who charge the amount covered by our insurance or negotiate the rate with the provider. Even though it takes a little more work on our part, it provides for all our healthcare needs and protects us from going bankrupt if any of us become ill or injured.

Chapter 44

Keeping Your Cash in Sickness & Health

Putting protection plans in place can be the very thing that saves you from a financial disaster. After the coronavirus closed non-essential businesses for almost two months, many businesses didn't survive. Small business owners who were unprepared for losing revenue for that long couldn't recover from such a significant loss.

They were forced to lay off employees, eat the cost of unused supplies or food gone bad, and had to frantically scramble to apply for small business loans and government-funded relief money before every other small business owner snatched it up. But the business owners who had been financially responsible and had saved three to six months of business expenses in an emergency fund before COVID-19 hit got through it unscathed and their businesses survived. Those business owners were able to pay their employees and themselves, even when their business was closed. They didn't need to experience the stress of filing for unemployment or applying for loans.

Those business owners also used the "time off" to come up with new, creative ways of providing better services to their clients and customers and developed innovative ways to meet the needs of people struggling through the pandemic instead of stressing and panicking over how to pay their mortgage. It was those people who stimulated the economy by supporting other small businesses because they had the money to do so.

No one was immune to the impact of COVID-19. It affected everyone. And no one is immune from future recessions, environmental disasters, illness, injury, and death. We're all at risk, but you can protect yourself and your money from these dangers and still come out on top when the going gets tough.

Money Therapy Assignment

Drafting Your Prenup

What kind of wine should we pair with drafting your prenup? I'm thinking a full-bodied red poured into a huge, fishbowl wine glass! Go grab it. Let's start this assignment by first visiting some wedding planning websites, scrolling through honeymoon destinations, and shopping for the perfect wedding gown just to add some fun.

After about ten minutes of "wedding planning," come back here and get started on drafting your prenup by mapping out what you're bringing to this money marriage. You're going to need to reference statements and other documents for accurate numbers. Complete this assignment wherever you keep that information.

Fill in the worksheet below to get a good sense of what you own, what you owe, and what your total net worth is (the difference between the two).

Assets (What You Own)
Cash on hand $_____
Cash in checking $_____
Cash in bank or credit union savings account $_____
Money market accounts $_____
Market value of your home $_____

Estimated value of household items $_____

Market value of other real estate (i.e. investment or rental property, timeshare, vacation home) $_____

Stocks $_____

Bonds $_____

Mutual funds $_____

Market value of vehicles (check<u>www.kbb.com</u> or <u>www.edmunds.com</u>) $_____

Cash value life insurance $_____

Current value of 401(k) plan or similar retirement account $_____

Individual retirement account (IRA, Roth IRA) $_____

Estimated value of personal items/other assets $_____

Total assets $_____

<u>Liabilities (What You Owe)</u>

Mortgage $_____

Home equity loan or line of credit $_____

Other real estate loans $_____

Auto loan or lease $_____

Credit card balances $_____

Student loans $_____

Delinquent taxes $_____

401(k) loan $_____

Personal unsecured loans $_____

Business loans $ _____

Life insurance loans $_____

Other liabilities $ _____

Total liabilities $_____

NET WORTH $_____ (Assets minus liabilities)

*Note: A net worth statement is a snapshot of the current value of your financial holdings. Keep in mind that the market value of your assets can change over time.

PART XI: LIVING HAPPILY EVER AFTER WITH YOUR MONEY

Chapter 45

Happily Ever After?

I hope by now you can see how far your money relationship has come. You've committed to your money, made promises to love and cherish it, and have been staying faithful by spending less and wiping out debt. Your money has been pulling out all the stops for you, and the more your money does for you, the more you swoon over it. Just like seeing your hottie wash dishes and vacuum can get you all hot (especially if it's done shirtless), seeing your money working for you to make your life easier is such a tease.

When you've got a real hottie on your arm, you wanna take 'em out and show 'em off. You want to shout from the rooftops that you're in love and show the world how amazing your sweetie really is. Same goes for your money honey. Your money is pretty special, you know. It deserves to be put to good use by sending it out into the world for everyone to see all the wonderful things it can do. It would be a real shame to keep your money all to yourself, hidden in a bank account, bored and lonely. You gotta take your money out!

Woah. Hold up. All you want to do is keep your money at home with you and binge watch episodes of *Love is Blind,* reminiscing about the days when you and your money were falling in love with each other. You want to spend all your time with your money and never be away from each other because you remember the days when money seemed so far away. It seems like just yesterday that money ghosted you, leaving you alone and scared. Because of bad past experiences, you still carry fear about losing your money, afraid that your money might walk out on you again in the future.

What if you get laid off and your income stops coming in? What if a major expense pops up, like your computer suddenly crashes or you get a massive bill for unpaid taxes that you didn't know about? All these worries about your money leaving you might make you want to clutch onto it, never let it out of your sight, and never let it go. "Please don't leave me!"

You might try to keep your money all to yourself, unwilling to share it with anyone else in an attempt to keep your money from ever leaving you. That's not healthy, boo. It's not good for you or your money relationship. This chapter shows you why being clingy and possessive of your cash is a bad thing (kind of a no-brainer but worth discussing anyway) and how to turn that crap around so you and your money experience a relationship filled with joy, trust, and a touch of magic! We'll also talk about how to use your money as an unstoppable force of good in the world through philanthropy, donating to organizations doing incredible work, and by using your money to make other people's lives better (and yours better too).

Your life isn't an episode of *Hoarders*. You don't need to stockpile money like people stockpiled toilet paper during coronavirus or stash money like a hoarder stashes twenty years of newspapers. Forget about penny-pinching to the extreme like those coupon clippers who spend four hours a week searching through weekly flyers to find the best deals and cataloging their coupons in big, fat binders so they can save fifteen cents on a loaf of bread. Ugh. The thought of living like that makes me feel like I've just ridden the Tilt-A-Whirl too many times.

If you love your money (and we know you do), you don't want to be a possessive, controlling partner. You wanna let your money come and go freely. Let it have "its own life," Let your money hang out with some other people once in a while without panicking and freaking out when your money chooses to have some time away from you. Absence makes the heart grow fonder after all. So, it's good for partners to take some time apart from time to time, and it's healthy for you and your money to have some time apart too.

Now, when I say it's good for your money relationship if you take some time away from each other, I'm not implying that you separate for months or you go cheating on each other. In literal terms, I'm not suggesting you intentionally stop doing things that will generate more income or that you go splurge at the mall. That's not what I mean by having time away from each other.

The healthiest way to let your money come and go freely is to be generous with it. Your money is awesome in so many ways. Why keep that awesomeness all to yourself? Share your money with the world! By sharing your money with other people, they'll get to enjoy your money, too.

It's just like when my hubby goes away on a fishing trip with his bros or I have a girl's weekend with my besties. My husband's friends get to enjoy him; we get some space from each other, and that makes us miss one another. When we come back together, my husband is all cuddly and smoochy, adoring the crap out of me.

Same exact thing happens with your money. When you let your money go hang out with other people and have some time away from you, it makes your money even more attracted to you, and it comes back all hot and heavy. In literal terms, the more you give, the more you get. The more you share your money by giving to others, the more money you'll attract back into your life. It seems contradictory, but that's how the Universe works. But first, you have to work through your fears of losing money before you'll be able to give generously.

Chapter 46

Money Fairy

CONFESSION: I was like a stalker with my money whenever there was a dip in revenue. I would seriously lose my shit whenever there was a lull in business or when my monthly expenses increased a bit. I'd get all suspicious about where my money was going. Why were the bills more *this* month? What was happening? I was like Joe from *You*, following my money around, tracking every tiny fluctuation in my bank account, and giving my cash the stink eye if it started to step out of line with my financial plan.

For such a long time, I had zero dollars. The struggle was real. I never, ever wanted to go back to the days where I worried about how I was going to pay the bills or saw huge balances and interest charges on my credit card statements. No way. I needed my money to stick by me, now and forever, and I never wanted to let it go.

I frequently flipped out on my husband, too. "I see you spent $3.12 at Sheetz yesterday. What did you buy? Did you really need that? Are you planning on spending that amount again tomorrow?" Any time Tom spent any money on anything, I'd run around like a chicken crying, "The sky is falling! The sky is falling!" I was driving myself nuts by being so hypervigilant about my money. I was driving everyone else around me bonkers, too.

Suddenly, I realized that having money was causing me just as much stress as *not* having it! Instead of feeling financial peace and contentment, I felt anxious and worried that all my money would suddenly disappear and I'd be right back to where I started. I didn't put in all the hard work of transforming my financial life to sit around worrying about my money leaving me. That would be a waste. I knew I needed to challenge myself to let go a little and "loosen the leash" on my money. But how?

That's when I got a wild idea. I mean, completely bonkers. I decided the best way to release the tight grip on my money was to give it away, like exposure therapy. The idea was to face my fears by totally immersing myself in the situation that provoked the most fear. I started walking around town, leaving $5 bills on random car windshields. Totally weird, right?!

OMG, I felt so uncomfortable every time I lifted a windshield wiper and tucked a bill under it. My mind kept screaming, "What the hell are you doing? You worked hard for this money, and now you're giving it away to random strangers? Have you lost your marbles?!" I crept through parking lots and hid behind cars as I spread my money around, hoping no one would catch me in the act or mistake me for a car thief. I had no idea what I'd say if someone asked me why I was leaving money on cars.

But the more cars I visited, the easier it was to leave the bills behind, and I started to think about how each person would feel when they found the money. I pictured the worn-out single mom coming out to her car after a long day at a job she hates, seeing that $5 bill and feeling so thrilled that she could treat herself to a Frappuccino on her way home.

I envisioned the young college kid, making minimum wage at a part-time job, working her butt off to get through school, and feeling like she never gets to do anything fun because she's broke as a joke. Then she finds the $5 and feels a sense of hope that maybe things are turning around and her luck has changed!

I thought about how happy each recipient would be and how that small amount of money could make a big difference in their lives, and that made ME so happy! The joy of sharing my money with the world made me want to skip through the parking lot, singing show tunes and throwing money everywhere. Like a magical money fairy, I pictured myself flinging fistfuls of cash as sweet joyful music filled the air. Then, everyone in town would come out into the streets with huge smiles on their faces. They'd grab handfuls of money and hug each other. Obviously, I didn't actually do that, but the fantasy was super fun.

Anyway, getting some practice sharing my money and being generous with it helped me to see that parting with my money really wasn't that scary. It also made me realize that money is meant to be enjoyed. It's meant to bless and help other people, to be shared and given space to flow in and out of my life freely.

A funny thing happened shortly after I started leaving money on windshields. I had a string of random events happen that returned that money to me tenfold. Someone paid for my order at the McDonald's drive-thru. Another person gave me a huge bag of fresh produce because she couldn't use it all before it went bad. A client who'd had an outstanding balance for six months finally paid their bill in full. Coincidence? I think not.

These were all examples of my money totally crushing on me, hugging and smooching me as we reunited, because I gave my money freedom and time away.

MONEY TRUTH: Lasting fulfillment doesn't come from what you GET. It comes from what you GIVE.

Does it feel good to make a shit ton of money? Hell yes. Does it feel like being snuggled up close with your sweetie in a warm, fuzzy blanket when you look at your hefty bank account? You betcha. But you know what feels even better? Making a massive impact on other people's lives by sharing your resources and gifts and adding tremendous value to the world. Knowing you made a difference and that you're leaving the world a better place than it was when you came into it is where the real joy comes from.

Once you find yourself in a solid financial position, where you're living debt-free, you've got your emergency fund fully stocked, you're making consistent income, and you're regularly investing for retirement, it's time to become a **magical money fairy**. As your Money Fairy Godmother, I hereby wave my magic wand and grant you your money fairy wings!

Now, go out into the world and sprinkle your money around like it's confetti. (After you finish reading the rest of this book, of course.) Throw that shiz everywhere! As you do, bless your money as it leaves your hands and goes into another's. Wish your money well, and picture all the amazing things your money will do while it's on the journey. Know and trust that your money will boomerang back to you in no time. Instead of clinging to your cash, hoarding it in a savings account, or worrying about when your money will return, take your money out and show it off.

Chapter 47

Take Your Money Out

I've got this little black dress hanging in my closet that I absolutely love. It's form-fitting, shows off my curves, and the plunging neckline makes me look like a foxy sex goddess. Every time I wear that dress, I feel amazeballs, like I own the place. And I never fucking wear it. Ever.

The poor thing hangs in my closet yearning to be held and touched while I wait for the perfect occasion to come along, and it never does. How about date night? Nah. It's not the kinda thing you'd wear to a casual dinner and a movie. A wedding? All my friends are married now. I haven't been invited to a wedding in years. Graduation party? Too sexy. Holiday party? Too cold.

As much as I love that dress and the way it makes me feel, I can never find a good use for it. So, there it sits, bored and lonely, waiting for someone to love it. For a long time, I treated my money the same way. Once I finally had more money than I needed, I didn't know what to do with it. So, I just stuffed it in a savings account and waited for the perfect occasion to pull it out and use it. Much like waiting for the perfect occasion to wear my little black dress, it never came along.

I always found some excuse or reason not to spend the money. So, it just sat in my bank account, bored and lonely, waiting for someone to love it, waiting for the idiot who put it there to wise up and use its power to change lives. That idiot was me. And eventually, I did wise up.

As a social worker who advocates for the underprivileged and believes strongly that we all have a responsibility to help people less fortunate than ourselves, this message held a special place in my heart, and it got me thinking about the world problems that really piss me off or make me cry. Any time I see those ASPCA commercials with abused animals gazing at me with their sad eyes, begging for someone to love and care for them, I bawl my face off. I just can't understand why anyone would hurt a helpless animal. It makes me so angry that I have crazy visions of hunting down the asshole who hurt that poor little kitty and burning their house down. But I know that torching someone's home isn't going to make things better. Instead, I decided to donate to the ASPCA every month because my money can and will help keep animals safe and rehabilitate those who've been hurt.

A similar thing happens when I see fundraising campaigns on TV for St. Jude's Children's Hospital. The thought of my own children being diagnosed with cancer brings tears to my eyes and imagining what our life would look like if we were fighting for their survival every day makes me want to throw up. There's nothing I can do to prevent my kids from getting cancer, but I sure as hell can use my money to fund cancer research and treatment in hope that lifesaving advancements will be made to help them or the other families who are currently living that nightmare.

When I started donating money to these organizations (and others) every month, I felt so good about it. I realized that my money needed a purpose aside from making my little life awesome. I discovered that my money is so much more powerful than I gave it credit for, and the perfect occasion to take it out into the world and put it to good use was **yesterday**.

I regretted not sharing my money with others sooner. I could have been contributing to important causes *while* I was paying off debt and building an emergency fund, and I probably could have worn my favorite little black dress to a bunch of different events had I not been so picky. With my newfound awareness, I experienced the joy and fulfillment of giving. It's something I'll *never* stop doing because my money deserves to go out into the world and be seen—not stuffed in a bank account or tucked in the back of the closet, waiting for the perfect occasion to come along.

Chapter 48

Be an Unstoppable Force of Good

Henry Ford said, "The highest use of capital is not to make more money but to make money do more service for the betterment of life." Money is the single most powerful tool you have, and if used well, it can make everything better, easier, and more interesting. Money can create wonderful options for yourself and others, right out of thin air. Money is like a magic wand. Wave that wand, baby!

In just a few simple steps, you'll have a plan in place for taking your money out, showing it off to the world, and giving it the opportunity to make magic happen in the lives of others.

Step #1: Look at your spending plan, and see how much money is available to give each month.

If you're still hitting your debt hard, you'll likely only want to devote a very small amount to philanthropy, and that's ok! Definitely prioritize your goal to become debt-free while helping as much as you can. Consider little luxuries you're willing to do without to free up money to help others. Is your weekly gel manicure more valuable to you than providing a month's worth of clean water to an entire village? How inconvenient would it be for you to cook dinner one extra night a week so inner-city high school students can receive contraceptives that reduce teen pregnancies? Decide how much money you want to devote to donations each month, and list it in your spending plan.

Step #2: Choose the organizations you want to support.

This might feel like an overwhelming process because there are so many awesome organizations doing incredible work in the world, but there are tons of resources to make the selection process simpler. The best place to start is to think about what problems or world issues get you really pissed off or make you bawl your eyes out (like I do over hurt animals and children with cancer). At the end of this chapter, you'll be exploring the causes that really set you on fire.

Step #3: Decide how much of your philanthropy budget you want to give to each organization you've selected.

Maybe you want to give all the money you set aside to one organization you absolutely love, or maybe you want to split it evenly among three non-profits. Maybe you want to give the most money to the organization most in need right now and less to the ones that aren't in a crisis. It's entirely up to you. An added bonus to donating money to philanthropic organizations is that you can write off donations on your taxes and reduce the amount you owe to Uncle Sam.

Schedule a money date, and talk it over with your money. Ask your money what project it wants to work on the most right now. Does it feel like sponsoring a child in Ghana so she can get adequate education and medicine? Does it want to work on an awareness campaign to register more people as organ donors? Or does it want to do both? Once you and your money make a decision, put it in writing in your spending plan.

Step #4: Set up automatic contributions to the organizations of your choice.

We've already covered why it's important to automate as much as you possibly can. Don't trust yourself to write the check every month. Set up automatic payments so you can contribute to worthy causes consistently without the hassle of remembering to do it each month.

If you're using YNAB for your spending plan, it will keep track of all contributions for you, but if you're not using budgeting software, you'll want to keep a spreadsheet of all the organizations you donate to and how much. These types of donations can be written off on your taxes each year.

Step #5: Consider getting involved and doing more than just writing checks.

You and your money can be a hero to people in need all around the world, but if you're low on cash right now, you really just want to buckle down and wipe out debt, or you want to experience even more joy and fulfillment than what comes from donating money, consider volunteering your time, talents, skills, and expertise to the organizations you want to support.

Money Therapy Assignment

Wave Your Magical Money Wand

Make a list of ten ideas about how you'll sprinkle around your money, time, energy, gifts, skills, etc. to practice letting your money flow in and out of your life freely.

Here are a few ideas to help you get started:

- Volunteer at a charitable organization, a church, or at your kid's school.
- Offer free advice to someone who can't afford to pay you right now.
- Tuck $1 bills in restaurant booths for the next customer to find.
- Pay your bills with joy knowing that your money is supporting other businesses and helping those employees support their families.
- Pay for the car behind you at the drive-thru.
- Give your server or bartender a really big tip for exceptional service.
- Skip a working lunch, and go have lunch with a friend who needs to talk.
- Make a big meal, and invite your neighbors over to share it with you.

- Donate your unwanted stuff, or sell it inexpensively at a yard/garage sale.
- Hire a college student to babysit your kids instead of leaving them with Grandma.

GREEN LIGHT! GO! Be as creative as you like. Give thought to sharing your money and resources with people and organizations you trust and respect. Sprinkle your money around like glitter!

PART XII: KEEPING THE SPARK ALIVE

Chapter 49

Happy Endings

Can you believe it?! You've reached the end. Whew! You've done a lot of hard work overcoming a history of money obstacles, scars, breakups, and make ups. You've tackled your money relationship problems head on and developed tools and skills to move you beyond ugly cries over an empty bank account to a new reality of earning what you deserve and managing money like a boss.

The skills you've developed at each stage of your money relationship are now the solid foundation of your money love affair—skills that you can use again and again for the rest of your life. The healthy financial habits that you've worked so hard to create will keep you and your money crushing on each other and living happily ever after.

So, does that mean we're done here? Is that it? You can just ride off into the sunset with your money, and everything will be peachy? In fairytales, once the lovers work through their shit and overcome the challenges that make their love story exciting and dramatic, the story ends with them holding each other close and sealing their love with a kiss. The scene fades to black, and we're left with that warm fuzzy feeling of a happy ending, trusting that everything worked out in the end and feeling satisfied with the conclusion of the story.

But your story isn't over yet. If fairytales were based on reality, there would need to be a sequel (or several follow-up stories) to tell the tales of what happens next. As life moves on, you'll return to previous stages of the money relationship, facing new challenges along the way. Complicated emotions about your money are bound to pop up again in the future.

You might revert back to old habits or unconsciously start sabotaging the blissful money love affair you've worked so hard to create. What are you supposed to do when problems resurface in your money relationship—ones you've never faced before? What's a girl to do when she feels overwhelmed and confused about investing? Who can she count on to help her through all the messy money drama? As our time together comes to a close, I want to show you how to use Money Therapy^R over time, so you're well prepared to handle any money relationship challenge that comes up in the future.

Chapter 50

Repeating Stages

You might be thinking, *Nah, Nicole. I'm good! I've totally got this whole money love thing. Living happily ever after with my money will be a piece of cake!* That's what I thought, too. Once I'd put in the hard work, turned my money relationship around, paid off all my debt, and socked money away for a rainy day, I thought I was set for life. I was in complete control of my money; I knew what I was doing, and I'd never go back to the toxic relationship with money I once had. But as I got more comfortable in my money relationship, I really started counting on my money to always be there for me, to love me even when I was being unlovable. After all, isn't that what marriage is all about? Unconditional love? For better or worse?

Because of this, I stopped being so obsessive about my money and relaxed. I became complacent. Money dates were less consistent, and I allowed myself to spend more on life's guilty pleasures. Money was meant to be enjoyed, right? I'd put in enough work. I deserved to enjoy the fruits of my labor. So, I started shopping more, just as a pastime, because it was fun, and I had the money to do it again.

I had fallen back to stage one of the money relationship, caught in the consumerism trap of spending money on shiny objects I didn't really want or need. When I realized I had returned to a previous stage and adopted bad habits, I was so pissed at myself. I should know better! Did I want to go back to pulling my hair out from money stress? Did I want to go deep into debt again? What was I thinking?!

Seeing how much money I'd spent on things that didn't really matter to me (again) was a wake-up call. The work on my money relationship wasn't over. I'd come a long way from the place I was in with my money before, but if I wanted my love affair with my money to last a lifetime, I had to keep tending to my money consistently *forever*.

Deep down, I knew this. I preached about it to my therapy clients, instructing them to keep working on themselves, their relationships, and their coping skills. I had to apply the same advice to my money relationship and just expect that there would be new issues to solve in the future. I had to recognize that old habits die hard. In order to stay true to my money and grow my money relationship stronger and stronger over the course of my life, I had to keep investing in my money relationship and devoting time and energy to maintaining it. I had to learn about money and ask for help. (Yes, even the "experts" need help. Every therapist needs a therapist.) I needed a financial therapist of my own. (More on what financial therapists do in a minute.)

I had to admit that my money relationship wasn't like the closing scene in fairytales. I wasn't going to seal my relationship with a kiss and run off into the sunset with my money, never having to do any hard work again. That kind of "happily ever after" is a myth. Once I realized that, I discovered what happily ever after *really* looks like.

Chapter 51

Happily Ever After Defined

Here's what "happily ever after" does NOT look like:

- All your problems are over.
- You've done all the work you need to do, and now it's smooth sailing.
- You'll never need help again because you've got this.
- You know everything you need to know until the end of time to live your best life.
- Your love is undying, unconditional, and forever protected from potential threats.
- You'll always have a swoon-worthy relationship because you love each other so much.
- You'll never make mistakes, revert back to bad habits, or do something to hurt the relationship.
- Your partner/money will never make mistakes, revert back to bad habits, or do something to hurt the relationship.

I hate to burst your bubble, but here's what "happily ever after" *really* looks like:

- Your current problems might be over, but new problems are inevitable. You need a plan for how you'll deal with them when they arise.
- You've done a ton of hard work, and there's still work to be done on your money relationship. There always will be.
- You've got this, and you'll definitely need help again in the future because you're growing and changing. With that comes uncharted territory you'll need help navigating.
- You know everything you need to know to maintain your current level of financial success, but if you want to level up your financial life, you've got a lot more learning to do.
- Your love for your money may be undying and unconditional, but there will forever be potential threats that can derail your money love affair and sabotage your financial success. Always be on the lookout!

You and your money love each other so much now, but like any relationship, it's not always sunshine and roses. You'll likely have negative feelings toward your money from time to time and may need help reconciling them. Unless you plan on doing nothing for the rest of your life, you'll be making a series of mistakes moving forward because that's how you learn and make progress toward your goals. You don't want to try avoiding mistakes. You just want to have a support person to help you work through them and figure out what to do differently/better.

Chapter 52

Money Relationship Maintenance

My job as a therapist is to work myself out of a job, which seems like a raw deal when it comes to job security, but that's how it is. When I work with couple's therapy clients, my one and only objective is to help them resolve the problems in their relationship, develop strategies and tools they can use over and over again, and get them feeling better about themselves and the relationship as quickly as possible. The goal is to equip my clients with the skills to manage life's challenges, their emotions, and their behaviors well on their own.

I do the very same thing as a financial therapist. This book serves as the first step toward transforming your relationship with money, increasing your income, gaining financial confidence, and securing your financial future. The programs, workshops, and consulting work I offer in my business dive even deeper into money management, strategic financial planning, and working through all the psychological and emotional barriers that sabotage financial success.

But here's the fact of the matter: Almost all of my clients over the past twenty years have gotten better, reached their goals, and experienced the results they were after. And almost all of those clients returned to therapy at some point later in time. Does that mean that therapy didn't work? Does it mean that they failed in some way? Does it mean that results are only temporary? No, no, and no.

It means that life is full of surprises. It means that sometimes the tools you have in your toolbox don't work for certain situations and you have to find new ones to solve the problem. It means that life is hard AF and sometimes you just need to vent about it, get a different perspective on the situation, and have some help figuring it all out. That's when you return to therapy.

As you move forward in your money relationship, you'll likely need Money Therapy^R again in the future, just like couples need the help of a therapist from time to time to give their relationship a little tune-up.

MONEY TRUTH: The best way to use Money Therapy^R is the same way you use car maintenance.

Think about it. When your car breaks down, you take it to a mechanic that you know and trust to fix the problem and get you back on the road. When your money relationship is broken, you take it to a financial therapist you know and trust to fix the problem and get you on track to have a healthy relationship with your money. But that's not the last time you'll ever see your mechanic. Once your car is fixed, you merrily go about your business, and you take your car back to your mechanic for routine maintenance and tune-ups to make sure everything is working right. You regularly care for your car to prevent breakdowns, so you don't end up stranded along the side of the road.

You should approach Money Therapy^R in exactly the same way. You are about to finish this book, but it won't be the last time you work on your money relationship or need the help of a financial therapist. Now that your money relationship is in a better place, your finances are on the right track. Still, you'll want to continue regularly tending to your money relationship and doing routine tune-ups with your financial therapist to make sure your money relationship is going the way you want it to. Proactively caring for your money, even when things seem to be going well, prevents financial crises, so you don't end up in a messy money divorce or financial disaster.

It's always a good idea to have a financial therapist on speed dial if problems pop up, so you can work through those quickly and easily without going it alone. Unlike financial advisors, financial therapists don't tell you what to do with your money or take over managing it for you.

Here's what financial therapists do instead:

- help you identify and work through your complicated thoughts and feelings about money so they no longer undermine your behaviors or stand in the way of your financial success.

- provide education about personal finance in layman's terms and empower you to make informed decisions for your money.
- empower you to take a more active role in your financial life instead of turning over financial decision-making to your partner, your dad, or your financial advisor. (*You* are the expert on your financial life, not anyone else.)
- show you how to develop a healthy relationship with money, shift limiting beliefs that keep you stuck, and guide you as you develop strong financial habits that will serve you well.
- help you create clear financial plans that align with your financial goals and serve as an accountability partner to cheer you on through the process of achieving them.
- serve as a non-judgmental support person who you can talk to openly about money shame, financial mistakes, and your hopes and dreams for the future.
- makes recommendations based on what would benefit *you* most, not yield big commissions for him/her/them.
- In other words, financial therapists are freakin' awesome. I personally believe every woman can benefit from having one. The sad part is that most women don't even know financial therapists exist! Like me, they've been trained to believe that they need a financial advisor or their financial life will spontaneously combust.

MONEY TRUTH: If you only focus on money management and what to *do* with your money and completely neglect the way you *think* and *feel* about money, your toxic money relationship will undermine your financial success.

    Financial advisors focus on money management, and that's an important part in creating a stellar financial life, but financial therapists get to the root of your money issues. They dive deep into the psychological and emotional issues keeping you from living your best financial life and solve money problems at the source so you can build a solid foundation.

    Instead of losing sleep for a week when an expensive financial surprise arises, you can consult with your financial therapist and work out a plan to turn the situation around. Instead of freaking out because you got an unexpected windfall of cash and you don't know how to put it to the best use, you can chat about it with your financial therapist and make informed decisions about how to put that money to work. Instead of feeling guilty and ashamed about getting caught up in retail therapy and consumerism again, you can work through those problems with your financial therapist and get the support, encouragement, and accountability you need to get back on track with staying faithful to your money.

    The best part of developing a close relationship with a therapist is that your therapist will always be there for you, no matter what. Because they know you so well, they can help you quickly conquer any financial challenge life throws at you. And you can bet your ass there will be challenges, ones you shouldn't have to face alone.

    Count on the fact that you'll revert back to old habits that negatively affect your finances at some point. It happens to everybody. Make sure you've got an accountability partner (like a financial therapist) to help you get back on track so you don't undo all the hard work you've done. Your money "will make mistakes and hurt the relationship" too. Like when the stock market crashes (hello, global pandemic that killed our economy) or when the investment you thought was smart turns out to be a waste of money (like when I realized my whole life insurance policy was a terrible investment). Make sure you've got someone to vent to when your money fucks up.

Long story short, happily ever after doesn't mean "the end." It means that a new chapter in your life is just beginning. The start of something exciting and different has just begun. New adventures await.

We have no idea what will happen next in your money love story, and that can be anxiety-provoking. What if you run into problems? What if you encounter new money demons that you've never fought before? What if your money does something that breaks your heart? You might be wondering, *What happens after I read the last sentence? What if I still have money issues I want to work through? How can I work with you and get the help and support I need to take my money relationship to the next level?*

I'm here for you, like a money fairy godmother, ready to help you fight any battle and win.

What if you want to take your financial life to the next level by creating multiple streams of income, so you can make more money while working less? Or what if you want to make savvy money moves by investing well so you can retire as a millionaire in less than ten years?

I'm here for you, as your trusted financial therapist, to guide the way.

What if you want to start a business, raise your rates, or ask for a raise? How can you deal with the imposter syndrome and feel fully confident that you deserve to make the money you want, without all the guilt or money drama? Who can help you sell more without being sleazy or salesy or help you gain the courage to ask your white-haired, good-old-boy boss to pay you what you deserve?

That's what I'm here for: to help you set even bigger goals for your money and bring them to life.

The book is coming to a close, but our time together doesn't have to end. We can keep this party going! Over the past several chapters, I think you've come to know me pretty well. I hope I've proven to you that my number one goal in life is to support your financial dreams, be your biggest fan, and hold your hand as you move through your money journey.

I'd love nothing more than to be there for you as you embark on this next chapter of your financial life. Learn more about my online classes, resources, and tools at www.nicolereneebooks.com.

It has been my deepest honor and pleasure to share my money love story with you and show you how you can start a love affair with money that will last a lifetime.

Congratulations to you and your money as you start your new life together! I hope it's filled with happiness and that all your financial dreams come true.

Money love & hugs (OO$O),

Nicole Renee

Acknowledgments

It takes a village to write a book, and I'm so grateful to all the people who helped bring *Money Therapy* to life. Thank you to my editor, Sarah Fox, for your time, skill, and thoughtful feedback to make this book the best it could be. To Emily Capuria, Jordan Eades, Michelle Glogovac, Becky LaBombard, and so many others who read drafts and made suggestions- thank you so much for your support and guidance. Thank you to the *Get It Done* team for creating the *Tiny Book Course* that guided me through every step of the publishing process. Deanna Seymour- thank you for this beautiful cover design. You nailed it! Cover photo credit goes to Tawnya Hemsarth Photography.

While I'm listed as the author of this book, I can't take full credit for this body of work. I'm merely the transcriber. This book was co-created by the Universe, my Spirit Guides, and myself. I feel honored to have been chosen to deliver this message to the world.

To all the amazing women entrepreneurs who have influenced my life's work and helped me build and grow my businesses- Crista Grasso, Diann Wingert, Susan Hyatt, Alexandra Franzen, Melissa Cassera, Shelley Cohen, Karen Hutton, Annie P. Ruggles, Laura Belgray, Jessica Dolgan, Marie Forleo, Danielle LaPorte, Amy Porterfield- thank you for your wisdom. It's inspired me to take big leaps.

I want to acknowledge and express appreciation for the many financial teachers and authors who taught me about money management, investing, paying off debt, and money mindset. Tony Robbins, Barbara Stanny, Jen Sincero, Dave Ramsey, Ramit Sethi, Tanja Hester, Kate Northrup, Mike Michalowicz, Farnoosh Torabi, and Bobbi Rebell (and many more)- your work is so important and so very needed.

A heartfelt thanks to all my newsletter & blog readers and current/former *Money Therapy*^{R} clients. Your emails, comments, sharing content, asking great questions, and commitment to transforming your financial lives makes my work feel like play. You're the reason I keep writing, creating, and teaching.

While writing this book, I lost two beloved members of my family; my mother and grandfather. I love them beyond words and miss them everyday. I can feel their presence and am grateful for the comfort that brings me. They, along with my grandmother, always encouraged me to go for my dreams and do what I love- whether it makes me money or not. I attribute my success as a writer to their unconditional love and support.

To my husband, best friend, teammate, and partner in all things, Tom- we've built a beautiful life together. Without you, I wouldn't be where I am today. It wasn't easy, but because of our hard work and commitment to each other, our life is everything I ever wanted it to be. Thank you for giving me the time and space to pursue passion projects and share our story with others.

Elan and Adley- I'm proud of this book but prouder of you. My greatest joy in life is being your mama. I hope that my financial experiences and the lessons I've learned help guide the way for both of you. No matter where life takes you, know that I'll always be with you and you'll always be loved beyond measure.

About the Author

Nicole Renee is a nationally recognized thought leader on money, business, mental wellness, and writing. She's been featured in *CNBC*, *Business Insider*, *Huff Post*, *Up Journey*, *Insider Inc.*, and *Elephant Journal*, as well as appearing as an expert guest on numerous podcasts. Audiences swoon over her psychology-based, outside-the-box approach to thinking about complicated topics in fun, simple, and relatable ways.

Nicole is a licensed psychotherapist with twenty years of experience working in mental health. She is also an author, entrepreneur, and real estate enthusiast. Nicole holds a bachelor of arts degree in psychology and a master's degree in clinical social work.

In her free time, Nicole devours self-help books, travels with her family, and savors coffee and gluten-free treats. Learn more about Nicole and her work at www.nicolereneebooks.com.

www.ingramcontent.com/pod-product-compliance
Lightning Source LLC
Chambersburg PA
CBHW020734020526
44118CB00033B/584